SKILLZ...
for the journey

Revel Pabon and Wynter Scott

BALBOA.
PRESS

A DIVISION OF HAY HOUSE

Balboa Press books may be ordered through booksellers or by contacting:

Balboa Press
A Division of Hay House
1663 Liberty Drive
Bloomington, IN 47403
www.balboapress.com
1 (877) 407-4847

Because of the dynamic nature of the Internet, any web addresses or links contained in this book may have changed since publication and may no longer be valid. The views expressed in this work are solely those of the author and do not necessarily reflect the views of the publisher, and the publisher hereby disclaims any responsibility for them.

The author of this book does not dispense medical advice or prescribe the use of any technique as a form of treatment for physical, emotional, or medical problems without the advice of a physician, either directly or indirectly. The intent of the author is only to offer information of a general nature to help you in your quest for emotional and spiritual well-being. In the event you use any of the information in this book for yourself, which is your constitutional right, the author and the publisher assume no responsibility for your actions.

Any people depicted in stock imagery provided by Thinkstock are models, and such images are being used for illustrative purposes only.
Certain stock imagery © Thinkstock.

Printed in the United States of America.

ISBN: 978-1-4525-2061-2 (sc)
ISBN: 978-1-4525-2062-9 (e)

Balboa Press rev. date: 2/18/2014

Dedication

Revel says …
To Alexis … thank you for inspiring me to live
in the moment. I love who you are.
To Marcus … thank you for your wonderful
imagination and personality.
You make me laugh.

~

Wynter says …
For my precious chosen children Dylan and Grey Braun …
I dedicate this book to you in hopes that you will learn to use
these SKILLZ and get the most out of your journey.

Contents

Preface

The issues facing our teens today are beyond scary. They can be dangerous and even life threatening. Sex, drugs, the dangers of social media, and bullying are just some of the struggles they are faced with each day.

The challenge … we all want to belong somewhere, fit in, and be validated. Sometimes we can find ourselves looking for answers to life's questions in the wrong places.

The solution … it takes SKILLZ to navigate through life's challenges. With so many choices, our young people can easily be overwhelmed by it all, looking only to the external world for value and self-esteem.

What is it that can help? Is it luck that they'll need to make the right choices, or do they already possess the SKILLZ they need to be successful? Our teens and young adults have real issues; they need real solutions. SKILLZ will give families an opportunity to discuss their thoughts and feelings on a vast number of topics that might not otherwise come up in conversation.

Communication is the missing link for young people, today. SKILLZ offers readers an opportunity to sort through the real issues they face and lead them on a journey to self-discovery through open communication and journaling, an opportunity to tap into the strengths that are inside us all. These SKILLZ will build self-esteem, giving teens the confidence they need to navigate through the tough spots successfully and celebrate their triumphs.

Acknowledgments

To our families ... thank you for loving us through this process.

Introduction

This book is designed to teach young people and their families how to utilize their inner strengths and good judgment in order to survive the day-to-day challenges of life. Common topics like school, family, and friendships are addressed as well as more sensitive topics like sex, drugs, the dangers of social media and bullying. Regardless of the issue, the solution comes from seeking help and looking within. Organized into 52 weekly chapters, this book serves as a starting place for daily family conversations by asking readers to answer questions on relevant topics that will allow them to explore new ways of coping and learning to rely on their own internal strengths.

This book is not intended to substitute for counseling, psychological or other mental therapeutic needs. If those aspects of help are needed please seek guidance from a professional in that field.

CHAPTER 1: *Honesty*

Being Honest Takes Courage

Being honest is one of the most valuable habits a person can develop. It takes courage to be honest with others especially if we're afraid of their reaction or how it might make us look. When we have to admit something that's embarrassing ... or address something that feels uncomfortable, it may first take a little time to gather up some courage. However, once we say it out loud, we usually feel better.

~

Is there something I need to be honest about?
Is there someone I need the courage to talk to?
What am I most afraid of?

~

Honesty without Love

There is honesty and then there is brutal honesty. There may be times we need to be honest with friends about something that might hurt their feelings. Maybe they're doing something that is dangerous or acting in an inappropriate manner and as their friend, we need to let them know. This can be challenging. Even the most painful truths can be said with love if we search for the correct words. That doesn't mean that they will like what we have to say. But if we say it with love, they'll know that it's coming from the heart.

~

Have I ever been "brutally" honest with someone? Why did I feel it necessary?
Has anyone ever been "brutally" honest with me? What was the result?

~

Honest and Humble

To be humble is to not be proud or arrogant. If we couple humility with honesty we will rarely go wrong. When we get confronted with something, our first reaction may be to respond with pride and ego by saying something like, "Yes, I said it, so what?" Or we may admit to it along with a list of excuses. These are both examples of *not* being humble. If there's something we need to be honest about, it's important to get our egos out of the way. This will make us people who are more approachable.

~

Why is it easier to approach a humble person?
Do I know someone who is humble?
What makes that person humble?

~

Honesty Creates Trust

The more that we practice being honest, the easier it becomes. After we've been honest with our friends and family on a regular basis, they will consider us trustworthy. This reputation is very important to have. It means that people will value and respect our opinion. It makes us credible.

~

Is there someone's opinion I respect? Why?
Is there someone's opinion I do not respect? Why?

~

Cash Register Honesty

Cash register honesty may be one of the hardest kinds of honesty to practice. It's harder to be honest when no one is looking. If a cashier gives us back too much change, or we find a piece of jewelry or a lost wallet, our first thought might be to stick it in our pocket before anyone notices. But that is definitely not the right thing to do. Doing the right thing when no one is looking will benefit us in the most powerful way. It builds self-esteem. And we can't put a price on that.

~

How would I feel if someone kept something that I lost?
How would I feel if someone turned it in?

~

Little White Lies

The term little white lie implies that a small lie is okay. However, a lie is a lie whether it's a big one or a small one. We may think that we can justify it, but the damage is the same. Often times, one lie leads to another and before we know it, we've told too many lies to keep track of. Remember that we don't get to pick our consequences. The price we pay for any lie isn't worth it.

~

What was the last "little white lie" that I told?
What was the last big lie that I told?

~

The Whole Truth

Some stories sound better if we leave something out or add something in for dramatic effect. This can happen easily if we are gossiping or trying to look cool in front of our friends. Once we have an audience it's easy for our egos to jump in and decide that the real story doesn't sound good enough. If we can't tell the whole truth, then we probably shouldn't be telling the story at all.

~

Have I been telling a story that isn't the whole truth? What is it?
Has someone told me a story that I suspect isn't the whole truth?
What story?

~

CHAPTER 2: *Positive Attitude*

It's My Choice

One of the coolest things we'll ever have is the freedom to choose. When we wake up each morning, we can choose to have a positive attitude regardless of what is going on around us. Think about it … would we rather be in a good mood … or a bad mood? The choice is ours. Even if we get sidetracked throughout the day, we can start our day over at any time with a positive attitude!

~

What kind of mood do I wake up with in the morning?
What kinds of things put me in a bad mood?
How can I change my reaction when negative things happen?

~

Being Responsible

Clean your room! Do your homework! Go to bed! We can get tired of being bossed around. Sometimes we can have really mean thoughts about the people who tell us what to do. That's normal. But … if we kept our rooms clean, did our homework on time, and went to bed without being told, no one would have a reason to "boss" us around! Think about it. When we do what we're supposed to do without being told, our lives will be much more peaceful. The choice is ours.

~

What things do I hate being "ordered" to do?
In what areas of my life am I irresponsible?
What can I do to become more responsible?

~

Perseverance

Perseverance is a big word. What does it mean? It means if we keep trying, we can achieve anything! If we have ever been asked to do something that we were almost positive we couldn't do, but tried anyway … that's perseverance. Sometimes life can be tough. When we lose a game, get a poor grade, or have a fight with a friend, do we run away and give up? Or stick it out and keep trying? When we stick with something, even if it's hard, that's perseverance.

~

What was the last situation I ran away from?
What do I think would have happened if I stuck with it?
When is it the hardest to persevere?

~

Positive Thinking

The power of positive thinking is very real. If we tell ourselves that something is too hard … it will be. If we tell ourselves that we can do something … then we probably will. Dream big and aim high. The worst thing that can happen is we'll have to try again. A famous quote of words to live by … "Think you can or think you can't, either way you will be right."

~

What are the goals I'd like to achieve? What must I do to achieve these goals?

~

Comparing Ourselves Now to Ourselves Then

Everyone does at least one thing really well. Some people do a lot of things really well. Sometimes we may feel bad because there's something we want to be good at, but there's always someone who seems to do it better. Comparing ourselves to other people can be painful. We should only compare ourselves to ourselves. If we really want to be good at something, then we must practice it regularly and in the end we'll probably find that we are better at it now than we were before. And then we'll be able to see how far we've come.

~

What are the things that I want to be really good at?
Who do I know is really good at these things?
How much am I willing to practice to get better?

~

Attitude Is Everything!

Attitude is everything. No one wants to be around someone with a bad attitude. No one enjoys negativity. When someone has a good or "positive" attitude, people respond in a positive way. When we have a positive attitude during a difficult time, people will respect us for the way we handle things. Attitude is everything.

~

What things do I need to change my attitude about?
Who do I know with a positive attitude?

~

A Work in Progress

We are "a work in progress" and that means we keep changing as we continue to grow, but we are not done yet. Sometimes, we may feel that things aren't happening fast enough. Sometimes, we may think that nothing is ever going to change. These are the times that we must remember we are … a work in progress. Maybe we are working on the things we'd like to change, but real change takes time so we need to be patient. Eventually, we'll see progress and when we look back we'll see how much we've grown.

~

What things do I want to change?
What things have I made progress on?

~

Chapter 3: *Kindness*

Being Kind—No Matter What

When we smile at someone, they should smile back. When we offer to help someone, they should say thank you. But sometimes people don't smile back or say thank you. When this happens....we may feel unappreciated or wish that we could take back our kindness. If our motive for being kind to someone is to get something in return....then we will probably be disappointed on a regular basis. It's important to remember that being a kind person is its own reward.

~

Have I ever been disappointed when someone didn't return my kindness?
How did I react to this feeling?

~

Kindness or Weakness?

Showing kindness to others is a simple gesture that speaks very loudly about a person's character. Some people may assume that if someone is always kind... then they can be easily taken advantage of. This is not true. Kindness and weakness are two different things. A strong person can speak kindly to others as they lay a boundary or address a difficult situation. It requires strength to take care of ourselves and even more strength to remain kind while doing it. This can be a very attractive quality that will go a long, long way.

~

Who do I know that is always kind?
Who do I know that tries to take advantage of kind people?
What do I think about these people?

~

Compassion

This is a special gift of the heart. But what is it? When we feel bad for the kid getting picked on … that's compassion. When we find a lost puppy and feel sad … that's compassion. Feeling compassion is one of those things that make us care about something that is outside of ourselves. But then what? Well, we could befriend the kid getting picked on. Or we could help the puppy find a home. These would be ways of showing our compassion.

~

How do I show compassion?
Who has been compassionate with me?
What are the things that I feel compassion for?

~

Compassion (a Little Deeper)

Compassion is a little harder to feel when we or a loved one has been hurt. When someone is being mean to us because he is having a bad day, do we feel compassion for him? Probably not! Maybe we are angry because now our feelings are hurt. If someone is mistreating us or a friend, we must try and look at the big picture. People who are happy don't yell and mistreat other people. So realizing that mean people are very unhappy people might help us understand why they are so mean. When we can practice compassion for the people who are not nice, instead of talking bad about them, we are definitely on the right path.

~

Who do I know could use a little compassion?
Why do I feel bad for them? How can I help them?

~

Cheer Someone Up!

Life is good! I'm having a great school year! I have a lot of good friends! When life is going well for us, it's a great feeling. But we mustn't forget to look around. Maybe someone close to us isn't doing so well. Maybe our mom and dad are going through a hard time with something. Or our brother or sister is struggling with school. It's a good idea to take some time to notice how the people around us might be feeling. Spreading our cheer around is one of the most loving things we can do. Caring for others will make us feel better about ourselves.

~

Do I know someone who could use some cheering up?
What could I do to make her (him) feel better?

~

Be Nice to Ourselves

Are we on our list of people to be nice to? Do we say nice things to ourselves or about ourselves? Hopefully we are as kind to ourselves as we are to others. Being kind to ourselves includes being gentle with ourselves … especially when we make a mistake. With all of the pressures of growing up (and we all know there are pressures), we need to remember to take it easy on ourselves. Give ourselves a break.

~

What are some special things that I can do for myself?
What are my best qualities?
When am I the hardest on myself? What can I do to change that?

~

Helping Out

Our parents probably do a lot for us. And they probably enjoy it. But what can we do for them? Instead of yelling out, "Mom, can you bring me a glass of water," we can get it for ourselves. When we see that the dishwasher needs to be emptied ... we can empty it! These things are pretty obvious. We are learning to do things for ourselves. But what about people who can't do things for themselves? Like a small child or an elderly relative. Should we leave that job for others? Or try to help out? Helping others who can't help themselves is the ultimate display of kindness.

~

Who needs my help today?
What can I do for them to help out?

~

CHAPTER 4: *Pride*

False Pride

Pride can very easily sneak up on us and turn into something ugly. False pride will make us lie to ourselves. We may believe that we are better than someone based on what we have, what we know, or even who we know. It's true that some people are better at certain things and some people have more than others. But that doesn't make them better people. Once we think we're better than someone else, we are in trouble. That is … false pride! No one has the right to judge anyone else. If we want to be proud of ourselves, we need to practice compassion, love, and understanding.

~

How do I feel when others judge me? What can I do with these feelings?

~

I Know!

Parents are always telling us what to do. Don't do that! Do it this way instead! Sometimes we may hear them tell us the same thing over … and over … blah … blah … blah. And what do we do? We say to ourselves … and even to them, "I know"! We roll our eyes. But some of the things that our parents are telling us now will be valuable information for us when we become adults. So we should pay attention! We can't let our pride stand in the way of listening to what someone else has to say.

~

What are some things that my parents keep telling me?
Why are they telling me these things? Why is it so hard to listen to them?
How could I respond without saying "I know"?

~

Apologies

When we apologize, are we truly sorry for our actions? Or do we have a list of excuses for our behavior? A true apology comes from the heart and shouldn't include phrases like "I'm sorry but…" or "I only did it because you….". If we are justifying our behavior while we are apologizing we will seem prideful and insincere. Mending a wrong and taking full responsibility for our behavior is where the freedom lies and the change begins.

~

Have I made any apologies that came with an excuse?
Has anyone apologized to me and blamed me at the same time?
What can I do differently next time?

~

Self Worth

We often feel differently about ourselves depending on whom we're hanging out with. There could be a group of kids that we feel lucky to be a part of, maybe so lucky that we never really feel good enough. Or perhaps there's a group of kids who we think are lucky to be hanging out with us. Either way, these are examples of our pride telling us what we are worth. And that's a very unhealthy way to live. If our feelings about ourselves change based on the group we are with, there is a good chance that we are judging ourselves based on what others think of us. If we feel "better than" or "less than" when we hang out with others, chances are we're not totally being ourselves in these relationships. When we are ourselves, we will feel comfortable in every situation.

~

Why do I feel lucky to hang around with certain people?
When am I comfortable being myself?

~

Family Pride

We all want to be proud of our families, but sometimes that's just not possible. We all struggle with making healthy choices each day. And some people do it better than others. When we focus on what others are doing wrong, (especially when it's a family member) we create a separation. It's important to remember that no one has the "perfect" family. We have to practice looking for the good in our family and being supportive when they need us. That's showing family pride.

~

When do I feel embarrassed about my family?
When am I proud of my family?
What can I do to be a more supportive family member?

~

Staying Humble

Pride is when we feel good about ourselves. But when we're not humble, we can push people away. If we do something totally awesome, and people praise us, it's important to stay humble and acknowledge everyone who helped us. When we try to take all the credit ourselves, people will immediately be turned off. It's very easy to turn something good into something bad if we're not careful.

~

When was the last time I took all the credit for something?
When have I given credit to someone else?

~

Life 'Just' Happens

As we go through life, situations arise. Sometimes we'll be pleased with the outcome and sometimes we'll be disappointed. It's not personal. Life 'just' happens. When we get attached to an idea of how things should be, our pride and ego can take over. We might become full of ourselves when we're happy with the outcome.......or so angry that we blame others if we get disappointed. Both of these are examples of pride and ego taking us into a danger zone. Not everything is good or bad...success or failure. When we can change our thinking to a realistic view we might find it much easier to learn from our mistakes and celebrate our achievements.

~

What have I learned from my most recent mistake?
What have I achieved that I am most proud of?

~

CHAPTER 5: *Mistakes*

A Whole Life of Learning

Everyone makes mistakes. Some people make the same mistakes over and over again. Some of us are really hard on ourselves when we make a mistake. The good news is that there is always something very valuable to learn from our mistakes. And since we can look forward to a whole life of learning, and we are bound to make mistakes, then isn't it better to learn something from our mistakes than to repeat them?

~

What are the areas where I make mistakes?
Who can I ask for help in this area? What have I learned?

~

Win or Lose

Most people enjoy playing games. But nobody likes to lose. Some people even get angry and give up. Yet if we do our best and have a good time, it's not as important if we win or lose. If we brag when we win and pout when we lose, we may find it hard to get people to play with us. People who are humble and gracious are always winners. Even when they lose!

~

How could I act differently when I lose?
How could I act differently when I win?

~

Good and Bad Choices

Most people know what good decisions are. But some of us choose to learn the hard way by making bad choices. And then we act surprised when we have to pay a price. When we know something is wrong and we choose to do it anyway, we really don't know how severe the price will be. But everything comes with a price! If we take the time to think about our choices and the consequences, we may be able to spare ourselves the pain that comes with the 'price tag.'

~

What was the last bad choice I made?
What was the price or consequence?
If I could go back, what would I do differently?

~

Second Chances

We know that we can't go back in time and change the past, but we do quite often get a second chance at things. Sometimes second chances present themselves right away, and other times a very long period of time might go by before an opportunity arises. Either way, whether it's a friendship, a problem at school, or simply achieving a goal, we can start thinking right now about what we'll do with our second chance.

~

What would I like to have a 'second chance' at?
What will I do differently?

~

Oops!

We all have regrets for something we've said or done. Maybe we borrowed something and accidentally broke it, or we said something offensive that we didn't mean to say. But is it fair to expect to be forgiven simply because we 'didn't mean to'? No. Whether a mistake is intentional or not, it's still a mistake. The other person is still entitled to his or her feelings about it. People will usually forgive us when we give them a sincere apology from the heart, without excuses.

~

When was the last time I did something that I didn't mean to do?
Did I apologize without excuses? Do I owe anyone an apology?

~

Judging Others

Some people make more mistakes than others. And it may seem that some people's mistakes are far worse than ours. But that is not our business. Nor is it our place to point them out to anyone else. The best thing we can do is to focus on our own lives, our own mistakes, and try to learn from other people rather than judge them. Unless what someone is doing is causing harm to someone, we should let them make their own mistakes and learn from them in their own time.

~

Who have I been judging lately?
Why do I feel the need to focus on their mistakes?
What have I learned from their mistakes?

~

Avoiding Mistakes

If we miss most of the questions on a test, we will probably get a bad grade. And we'd deserve it. If we didn't study or put in the work, we're not entitled to a good grade. But before we beat ourselves up, we need to think about this. We will get as much out of something as we're willing to put into it. If we want to avoid making mistakes, then we need to study hard, do the work, and think about our choices before we make them. Mistakes are a part of life. But when we try really hard to do our best, they can sometimes be avoided.

~

What should I be studying more?
What do I 'beat myself up' over?
Who can I ask for help?

~

CHAPTER 6: *Acceptance*

Why Can't Things be Different?

Wouldn't it be nice to live in a castle or a palace? Or how great would it be if we had every game and nothing but time to play them? Wouldn't it be awesome to eat whatever we wanted all the time? Yeah … right! Only kids in fairy tales live like that. In the real world, we live in houses or apartments, only have a few games and eat what's put in front of us! And guess what? That's exactly the way it's supposed to be. As we learn to accept the structure of our lives, we appreciate the little things so much more.

~

What is easy to accept about my life?
What do I have trouble accepting?
Why do I think things should be different than the way they are?

~

Goodie Goodie

We might know others who are never in any trouble and do everything right. We wonder how they do it. We can wonder forever and never come up with an answer. Nobody does *everything* right. It just appears that way sometimes. When someone is good at something, it looks easy. We all have special SKILLZ and talents. The more we focus on how well someone else does something, the less we will appreciate our own talents. We should accept who we are and be happy for others.

~

In what areas am I really skilled?
In what areas would I like to improve my SKILLZ?
Who can help me get better in these areas?

~

When I Grow Up ...

We've probably all heard, "You can be anything you want to be when you grow up." This is true as long as we possess the abilities needed to achieve our goal. Unfortunately, everyone has limitations. For instance ... if we want to be a doctor, we have to have the grades to get into medical school. Without the grades, it will never happen. But that doesn't mean we can't do something else in the medical field. Knowing our limits is one way to practice acceptance in our lives. Once we know and accept who we are ... we are free to pursue our dreams.

~

What do I want to be when I grow up?
Do I have any limitations?
What can I do to work around those limitations?

~

Perfection

Striving to be perfect is a sure set up for disappointment. No one is perfect. We should accept ourselves and each other for who we are, with all our imperfections. If we are unhappy with something about ourselves that we can change, then we can work on it. But in the process, we should accept who we are as we are and love ourselves.

~

What is it about myself that I like just the way it is?
What would I like to work on?

~

Blended Families

There are many ways to make up a family. Our mother or father may be a "step" parent. Or perhaps we have a step-brother or sister. When we look at other people's families, ours may appear to be different or even weird. The truth is, no matter who they are, if they live together and love each other, they're a family. We must learn to accept that our family is special and perfect just the way it is.

~

What do I love about my family?
What do I think is *strange* about my family?
What would I like to do more of as a family?

~

Living with Feelings

Some things can be really, really hard to accept. Like not being invited somewhere, or being talked about behind our backs. These are things that most of us have a hard time getting 'okay' with. But the truth is, we don't have to like something or be okay with it to accept it. To accept something means to acknowledge it, define it, feel it, and then go on with our lives. Once we accept something we may still feel hurt, but that cannot stop us from doing the next right thing … whatever that may be. Feelings can change, and the change starts with acceptance.

~

When was the last time I got my feelings hurt?
Have I accepted what happened and moved on?
If not … why not? If so … how did I do it?

~

It Is What It Is

Those 5 little words pack a powerful punch. They can change our whole life. When we can look at a situation and accept it as it is, we can free ourselves from emotional pain. It's okay to want things to be different…but when we try to fight the way things already are, we set ourselves up for a struggle. No matter what it is that is bothering us… regardless of how big or small it may be…we can find peace in acceptance.

~

What situation have I had trouble accepting?
What situation have I found easier to accept?

~

CHAPTER 7: *Patience*

... Is a Virtue

A virtue is a good quality in a person. Patience is a virtue not only because it is a really good quality, but because it's also a really hard quality to master. When we roll our eyes waiting in line, get angry when someone isn't moving quickly enough for us, or get frustrated waiting for our project to be completed ... we are far from being patient. When we can be peaceful inside and have acceptance that some things just take a little longer, we're practicing patience.

~

Why do I think patience is important?
Whom do I need to be more patient with?
What areas of my life do I need more patience?

~

Rock Solid

A sure sign that we're maturing is when we take our time to do our best, when we care enough to make sure there is a "rock solid" foundation underneath whatever it is that we're building. Everything from a school paper to a new friendship, deserves our undivided attention. When we try to do things without taking shortcuts or rushing through them, things generally tend to turn out better.

~

What areas in my life need a rock solid foundation?
What areas have I already built a rock solid foundation?
Why is it important not to take shortcuts?

~

Take Our Time

When we rush through our homework … we'll probably end up with a mistake or two. When we rush through our chores … we'll probably end up forgetting something or doing a sloppy job. If we rush through meals, we might end up with indigestion. The point is that when we rush through life, we might end up doing a lot of things over again or worse, we might miss something really special. When we take the time to get it right the first time, we get the benefits of a job well done.

~

What have I rushed through lately? Why am I rushing?

~

Using Our Time Wisely

When we feel 'inconvenienced' because we have to wait for something, that can mean one of two things: either we think that our time is so much more important than everyone else's that we shouldn't have to wait, or we are not using the time to our advantage … or maybe a little of both. There are a lot of valuable things that we can do while we wait. We could carry homework or a book. Maybe keep a notebook handy so we can journal or make a list of the things we'd like to get done the next day. Instead of getting annoyed … we can get creative! We can use our time wisely.

~

When do I spend the most time waiting?
What can I do to use my time more wisely?
How can I benefit from this change?

~

Teaching Patiently

A good teacher will have a lot of patience. Because everyone learns at a different pace, a good teacher will not get frustrated with the kids that take a little longer to catch on. If we've ever taught a dog to sit or showed a three-year-old how to tie his shoes and can do these things without gritting our teeth or raising our voice when they don't get it right away … that's teaching patiently. When we can do these things and actually enjoy and appreciate the experience … we understand what it means to have patience.

~

What do I find frustrating to teach to someone else?
Why does it frustrate me?
What took me a long time to learn?

~

In Friendships

All friendships have ups and downs. Even our closest friends … the ones we love to hang out with can drive us crazy sometimes. Just like with our family, we need to practice patience with our friends. This will help us get through those rough spots. No judging, no yelling, no running … just patience. Exactly the same way we'd like them to treat us.

~

Who is patient with me?
Do I owe any apologies for my lack of patience?
If given the opportunity, what would I say?

~

Don't Lose It!

It's easy to lose patience with people. When people aren't acting the way we think they should be acting, or doing things the way we think they should be done, our reaction to them will say a lot about what kind of people we are. We can either lose patience and try to control them, or practice patience and accept them. When we expect people to do things our way, we will surely be let down. When we are patient and accept people, we get to be supportive of them … and we get to be proud of ourselves for not losing it.

~

Why do I think things should be done my way?
When was the last time I 'lost it' on someone?
What are some changes that I'm now willing to make?

~

CHAPTER 8: *Serenity*

A Peaceful Life

Serenity is about *creating* peace in our lives. Sometimes, we just have a peaceful life … other times we have to create it for ourselves. Maybe we got into an argument with someone, but we can't do anything about that now. We can't change the past, but maybe next time we can handle it differently. When we look for solutions to our problems, we can make a difference in how things turn out the next time. And that can reduce the drama in our lives.

~

Is there someone I need to apologize to?
Do I need to forgive someone?
What can I do about the drama in my life?

~

Good Intentions

Most people want to do the best they can, which means they have good intentions. When we start each day with good intentions, our chances of having serenity are much better. We know that no one is perfect and life doesn't always go our way … and that's okay. We cannot control how things turn out each day. But we can practice serenity even when things don't go as planned. Good intentions bring about good things and a happy spirit.

~

Do I have good intentions each day?
What kinds of things are out of my control? What do I try and do about it?

~

Life is a Journey

"Life is a journey, not a destination." If we spend our time saying things like "when I get … then I'll be happy," we might be spending too much time focused on tomorrow. When we live each day only focused on tomorrow, we lose the value of the moment. Planning for the future is a good idea but it shouldn't be the only idea. 'Life is a journey' means that we spend each day living, loving, and learning to enjoy it all. Tomorrow will take care of itself when it gets here.

~

What am I waiting for that I think will change my life?
What can I do to learn to stay in the moment?
What's the difference between planning for the future and depending on it?

~

Don't Sweat the Small Stuff

"Life" happens every day. Rarely will everything go the way we planned. And that can be frustrating. But that's life. If we let every little disappointment frustrate us, we could spend a lot of our life frustrated and disappointed. Instead, we should look at the bigger picture in life. When we think about how big the world is, it's easier not to let little stuff bother us. Remember, we get to decide what bothers us. We also get to decide what we are *not* going to let bother us. It's our choice.

~

What are the "little things" that bother me? Why do I think that is?
What are the "big things" that bother me? How are they different?

~

Stay Focused

Serenity comes from within. It's not necessarily about being in a peaceful *place*. It's about being calm and relaxed on the *inside*. Keeping calm amidst chaos is a skill. And we can practice this skill by breathing in and out and staying focused. When we can learn to focus our thoughts and quiet our minds, we begin a process of monitoring what we let into our world. So, just because it might be a crazy day doesn't mean we have to buy into it. We can remain calm on the inside.

~

When is it hardest for me to focus?
What's the best place in my house to get quiet and 'just breathe'?
What's the best time of day to practice these things?
Am I willing to try this regularly?

~

Enjoy Today

The past is gone and tomorrow is not yet here. So all any of us have is right now. We can learn from the past but we don't want to live there. Tomorrow can hold promises but we can't live there either. Learning to enjoy today is something we can practice. There is serenity in the moment. We can start by being aware of how much time we spend thinking about the next day or yesterday. When we catch ourselves doing that, we should remember to focus on what we are doing right now, and live our lives every day enjoying the gifts we have been given.

~

How much time do I spend thinking about what happened in the past?
Do I spend all of my time daydreaming about tomorrow?
How do I show appreciation for each day?

~

Feed Our Souls

Finding things in our lives that make us feel better should include things that focus on our serenity. Maybe we are interested in a spiritual path. Maybe it's the outdoors that helps us connect with life. We need to do something for ourselves to feed our souls. Our serenity depends on it. Some people go to church. Some people love to hike and be with nature. Others meditate. Whatever it is, it needs to be personal. It needs to be something just for us.

~

What do I do for my serenity? Is it something I do every day?
Can I think of some new things to do?

~

Chapter 9: *Strength*

During the Storm

Keep a cool head … stay calm … don't panic. These are valuable pieces of advice. Practicing these during an emergency has literally saved lives. It helps people make sound decisions during times when they might be really excited or too emotional to think straight. How do we do this? Count to ten, take a deep breath, or take a few steps back. The whole point is to remain level-headed. Otherwise, we can make a bad situation worse. Even at a moment when there's only a split second to think … one level head is far more effective than several emotional ones.

~

When was the last time I panicked? What was the outcome of that situation?
Who in my life would I describe as calm and strong?
How would they have handled the same situation?

~

Unite Our Minds, Bodies, and Spirits

Our physical strength might depend on how well we take care of ourselves. Our mental strength also can depend on the workout that we give our minds. And our spiritual strength can grow, too, if we pay attention. This is how it works. Our minds, bodies, and spirits all need workouts. To grow as a whole person we need to do more than eat right and exercise. We need to nurture all of us. And that includes our minds and spirits.

~

How do I nurture my mind? Do I read? Do I write?
What are some other ways to nurture my mind?
How do I nurture my spirit? Do I practice yoga? Do I go to church?
What are some other ways to nurture my spirit?
What are my strengths?

~

Feelings

Some people are afraid to acknowledge their feelings. But our emotions are part of being human and it is okay to feel them and show them. It doesn't mean we are weak. What we don't want to do is react to them. And that is different from showing them and feeling them. It's okay to feel our feelings.

~

What is the difference between 'showing' my feelings and 'reacting' to them?
What feelings are the hardest for me to feel?
What feelings are the hardest for me to control?

~

Superhero

Who doesn't love a great superhero? A made-up character on the big screen in Hollywood, we fall in love with them and idolize them. But as we grow up and mature, we tell ourselves they're not real, it's all fake. There is no such thing as a superhero. But is that true? Maybe our definition of a superhero might be on a set in Hollywood. What if we brought it a little closer to home? What does it take to be a superhero? It takes a person who can really help those who need it, someone who doesn't let fear stop them. We all have the potential to be superheroes even if we only do one thing in our lives that helps someone. That can make us a superhero at least to the person we helped! So we might not be flying around with a cape and magic powers, but we can all help someone... probably much more than we ever imagined.

~

Who has been my real life 'superhero'?
What did he or she do to help me? How can I return the favor?

~

Power

Power can be awesome. It's exciting to watch a 'powerful' person in action. We all have power inside of us. We simply need to discover where our power lies, harness it, and apply it to an area that we're passionate about. That means focus on something we really want to do with our lives and put our efforts there.

~

What am I passionate about?
Where does my power lie? What am I really good at?
How can I put these together to build a strong foundation for life?

~

Beyond Our Control

When we think of strength we probably don't think of "doing nothing." But sometimes acceptance means just that. And it takes a strong person to do nothing. When things aren't going our way, do we want to try and fix it or control it? Or are we able to recognize that it might be something that we need to leave alone? Accepting when things are out of our control and that we should do nothing requires a lot of strength.

~

What things are out of my control?
What situations have I tried to control anyway?
What was the outcome?

~

From the Inside Out

Are we people who never crack under pressure? Some of us hold it together during the big game; keep calm during a big test; don't let our emotions control our actions. If our actions are guided by our practical nature and not our emotions, we will save ourselves and others a lot of frustration … just by being us.

~

Have I ever been the 'calm' in the middle of the storm? When?
What are the benefits of this kind of strength?
What are the consequences when I don't have this kind of strength?

~

CHAPTER 10: *Peace*

Peace on Earth

This is a saying of hope. It means that many people hope for a day where there is peace on this planet. Although it may seem like a far-off dream to some, we can do our part to help this dream come true. Peace is something that exists when people try to understand and respect each other. People will always disagree … but it's what comes after disagreeing that creates peace or a lack of it. When we try to see another person's point of view, without the need to be right, we can have peace even if we don't agree.

~

How do I react when I don't agree with others?
Do I argue with them until they see it my way?
Why is it so hard to 'let go'?

~

Balance

Sometimes it seems like there just isn't enough time to do everything. Some of us are so busy that we appear to be constantly 'on the go' every day. When we find ourselves tired, stressed out, and no longer enjoying our lives, then we're probably out of balance. Rest, relaxation, and down time, are just as important as school, activities, and socializing. Create a place for these things. Create balance, and our lives will happier. Balance can add peace to our lives.

~

What can I change to create more balance in my life?
Am I afraid of missing out on something? Why?

~

Drama

Are we all about drama? If a lot of our conversations with friends tend to revolve around what someone else did or said, we might want to take a look at our attraction to drama. If what we're saying about someone can't be said to his or her face, then we probably shouldn't be saying it. It's one of the oldest golden rules to live by. We can choose to create peace in our lives, or we can choose drama.

~

Why is it unhealthy to have drama in my life?
Do I trust people with a lot of drama in their lives? Why or why not?

~

Peaceful Learning

Getting in trouble is no fun. It happens to everyone. It's a part of growing up and it's how we learn right from wrong. Some of us may have to learn the same lesson more than once. If we find ourselves acting out in a behavior that keeps getting us into trouble, we're probably not feeling very peaceful. Peaceful learning means we only need to learn a lesson one time to become willing to change. It's possible.

~

What is the worst thing I've gotten into trouble for?
What did I learn from the experience?
Have I done that again? Would I do it again?

~

What Can I Do?

We can make a difference in this world if we are willing. It starts with helping others. Even the smallest gesture can bring peace to someone else. If we're not sure what we can do … we ask someone. We observe the people in our lives who clearly help other people. We watch the reaction of the people they help. We'll see that it feels just as good to the person offering help as it does to the person receiving it.

~

How can I help create peace in someone's life?
Who would I like to help?
Who was the last person to help me? How did that person help?

~

A Peaceful Life

How great it is to have a day where we laugh and hang out with people we care about. That sounds pretty peaceful, doesn't it? Although every day will not be peaceful, there's nothing wrong with wanting it to be that way. We can do our part by being nice and respectful to everyone. We can create a peaceful environment all by ourselves. Peace is created one person at a time.

~

What can I do to help make my day peaceful?
What was my most peaceful day like?

~

Dreams

Dreaming of a life we think we want is something all of us do. However, keeping our dreams based in reality may be the tougher challenge. Wishing for a life that most likely isn't possible can leave us feeling disappointed and empty. Dreaming of a life that pushes us out of our comfort zone, but is realistic, may be a better approach to achieving our dreams. What do I daydream about? Are my dreams achievable?

~

What do I daydream about?
What are my 'night' dreams usually about?
What does being peaceful mean to me?

~

CHAPTER 11: *Manners*

Appropriate Behavior

Our society is based on appropriate behavior. There are rules and laws aplenty! Because this society demands appropriate behavior, life is much easier when we get along with each other and treat each other with respect… even when we disagree. Appropriate behavior will help us to attract the kind of people that we want to be around. Unfortunately inappropriate behavior can attract bad situations. It's important to be aware of our actions at all times.

~

Has my behavior been inappropriate?
How does that affect my life?

~

Me—Version 2.0

Our computers, smartphones and tablets all have filters. Filters keep the operating systems free of viruses. Viruses are the 'bugs" that can damage our devices. Viruses can also damage our relationships. So, the question here is… do we have a filter? Do we think before we speak? Do we consider someone else's feelings before we blurt out our opinion? Having a filter means we let someone else finish their thought before we cut them off. We stop and think before we speak. We consider what we are about to say before we say it. We ask ourselves if what we are about to say will be helpful, kind and loving. We speak from the heart, not from our ego.

~

Do I listen first, and then speak?
Why is it important to filter what I say to others?

~

Being Helpful

When we carry in the groceries, it shows that we want to be helpful. When we hold the door open for someone who's coming in behind us, we're being courteous and helpful. Our behavior affects other people. Being helpful shows we care. Remember, we don't have to wait for someone to struggle … before we offer to help.

~

What can I do to be more helpful?
What do I already do … to show I care about others?

~

Excuse Me

When we walk in front of someone, we should say "excuse me." When we burp, hiccup, or even worse … we should say "excuse me." If we need to interrupt someone's conversation to speak, we should say "excuse me." When we have to get up from the table in the middle of dinner, we should say "excuse me." These two simple words can be the difference between being polite and being rude. Being polite shows that we realize what we do and say affects other people. It means we have respect for others.

~

Do I say "excuse me" at the appropriate times?
Do I find it funny or cool when people don't say excuse me?
Why or why not?

~

Being Polite

As children, saying "please" and "thank you" are usually the first manners we are taught. Parents try to teach their children the importance of being polite because they want them to be socially accepted. However, there is so much more to being well-mannered than simply saying "please" and "thank you." There are things like … patiently waiting our turn, listening without interrupting someone and apologizing when we're wrong. They all count in the end.

~

Do I consider myself a polite person? Why or why not?
What are some manners I need to work on?

~

It's the Thought That Counts

We all love to receive gifts and feel special because someone thought of us. And hopefully, the gift is something we'll totally enjoy. But whether or not we like what we've received, it's far more important that we see the real gift, which is the thought. Being gracious and kind are two of the most honorable ways to show good manners. Regardless of the gift … if someone thought of us … we can say "thank you," and hopefully, mean it!

~

Do I graciously accept all the gifts that I'm given?
Is there anyone I might need to thank?

~

Being Considerate

Some people like to tease their friends about the way they talk or dress. It starts out as fun and then someone crosses the line. Teasing hurts people's feelings, even if it's just for fun. It's inconsiderate … especially when it's happening to us. When we think about what we are saying and how it might make someone else feel, we are less likely to hurt someone's feelings. Respecting others and teasing people rarely can be done at the same time. They just don't mix. Having good manners and respecting others means being considerate of the people in our lives.

~

What was the last thing I was teased about?
Who was the last person I teased?
What does the word 'considerate' mean to me?

~

CHAPTER 12: *Willingness*

Earning Our Way

How many times have we seen something we wanted only to hear our parents say, "we can't afford it"? If we had our own money, we might be able to buy it on our own. There are a lot of things that we can do to earn our own money. We could walk people's dogs, babysit, deliver newspapers, mow lawns, wash cars, or clean out garages. We can start in our own neighborhood, help people out, and earn some money at the same time.

~

What would I buy if I had my own money?
What can I do to make my own money?
Am I willing to work hard for what I want? Why or why not?

~

Don't Give Up!

Sometimes things don't go as planned. When we get disappointed, it's normal to want to quit. Quitting is easy, but then what? Before we quit, we'll want to make sure that we gave it our best. Otherwise we may end up wondering what might have happened if we hadn't given up. When we work hard at something and do our best, we build strength, character, and most importantly … we'll prove to ourselves that we have the willingness to do what it takes, no matter what.

~

What have I started that I eventually gave up on?
Why did I quit?

~

Follow Through

Some of us are great starters, but when it comes to finishing things … sometimes that's not so exciting. When we lose our momentum and let some time go by without working on something we've started, a day or two can easily turn into a week. And before we know it, a whole month has gone by. But being a "follow-through person" doesn't have to be so hard. We can find the same excitement about a project that has been sitting as we can with starting a new one. Sometimes we have to pretend to be excited about it until the original excitement shows up again. Chances are it will, especially when we complete the project. We need to show our willingness and follow through. We'll be glad we did.

~

Am I a follow-through person or just a good starter?
Do I know someone who always follows through? What can I learn from her (him)?

~

Our Will

Our "will" is that little voice inside that guides us. It's always better if our will is in line with things that are good for us. It's not always like that, though. Sometimes our will has a mind of its own and it can lead us right down a path of destruction. So, how do we know when to act on our will and when not to? We won't always know ahead of time. But we can show willingness by taking some time to ask others what they think. Getting a second opinion may save us from pain later on. In the meantime, we have to remember that just because our thoughts tell us to do something doesn't mean that we have to do it.

~

Who in my life can I go to for a second opinion?
When have I acted on my will and then regretted my actions?
How far have I gone to get what I want?

~

Something New

Trying something new can be scary. But we don't have to let that stop us. If we are willing to walk through our fears, we might find that there are a lot of different things we enjoy. We need to ask ourselves this question: If I try something new and don't like it … what is the worst thing that would happen? Trying to answer this question might give us courage when we realize that the worst of our fears aren't that bad.

~

When was the last time I tried something new?
What happened after I tried it? What else would I like to try?

~

Something Old

There are times in our lives when we know we are ready for a change. Maybe it's time to change some old habits, get rid of something and start anew. When we want to make a change in our lives, it's best to have a plan. It helps to be clear about what we want to change and then be clear about what we'll do differently. We also need to have the willingness to try the new thing when we want to do the old thing. It takes time to make a new habit and break an old one. We have to be gentle with ourselves … but stick with it.

~

What are my bad habits? What are my good habits?
What habits cause me pain?
What am I willing to do to change?

~

Action

Willingness has to be accompanied by an action to really be willingness. What does that mean? We can want to do something wonderful with our lives, do some really fun things, be someone who can make a difference, but unless we stand up and get moving, none of those things are likely to happen. So, wanting to do something and actually doing it is the difference between daydreaming and reality.

~

What am I willing to take action on and do?
What am I not willing to take action on? Why not?

~

CHAPTER 13: *Sharing*

In the Moment

We've all had special moments with a best friend. Sometimes we feel so close to that person it seems like it will always be this way. But people will come and go in our lifetimes. As we grow up, our interests change and our friends change, too. That's why it's so important to enjoy the moment. Learning to embrace the moment we are in is the most precious gift of life. So, even though people change and move on, we can remember the special moments in our hearts forever.

~

What is one of the most special moments that I can remember?
Who have I shared the most special moments with?

~

A Two-way Street

If we find ourselves in a friendship that feels one-sided, it can't be healthy for either person. A friendship where one person is 'in-charge' all of the time isn't balanced. A true friendship should be a two-way street. For instance, some days we might make all the decisions and on other days, it's the other person's turn to make the decisions. When two friends can come together and compromise on a decision, there is a nice balanced flow and the friendship is a two-way street.

~

Have I ever been in a friendship that felt one-sided?
Who are my true friends?
What makes these friendships healthy?

~

It's Mine!

Sharing our stuff doesn't always come naturally. We get attached to our things and want to keep them to ourselves. That's our ego hard at work. The ego wants to keep everything for itself. It's mine! But sharing can be a great way to be nice to a sibling or a friend. It's a perfect way to think of someone else for a moment. When we share with others we are actually practicing humility. It diminishes the ego. As we get older, sharing usually turns into helping. And helping someone can make us feel good about ourselves and it's a great way to lead by example.

~

What are the things I find easiest to share? Why?
What are the things I find harder to share? Why?

~

Ourselves

People love to get gifts! And many people love to give gifts! Giving and receiving gifts feels good. Most people think that a gift has to have some monetary value, but the most precious gift we can give someone is ourselves. How do we share ourselves with someone? We can share the gift of 'ourselves' by being a friend, helping them when they need help, by spending time with them and by being a good listener. Showing we are interested in them is a great way to share ourselves.

~

Who would I like to spend more time with?
How can I share more of myself with my family?
How can I share more of myself with my friends?

~

Lending Our Stuff

A golden rule about lending stuff is realizing … we may never get it back. So before we lend something to someone, we need to ask ourselves this question … if I never see this 'thing' again, am I okay with that? And if we can answer yes, then we are lending with an open heart. If we cannot lend with an open heart, then we are better off not lending at all. We will actually be doing everyone a favor by saying 'no.' It's okay.

~

Is there something that I'd rather not lend? What?
Have I ever lost or ruined something that someone lent to me?

~

Trusting Someone

Sharing our private thoughts and feelings can be uncomfortable. Everyone needs at least one person that they can trust to share their deepest thoughts with. Unfortunately, not everyone is trustworthy so we have to be careful before we open up to just anyone. Sometimes the only way to know whom to trust and whom not to trust is to take a risk. Follow our instincts and hope for the best.

~

Whom do I trust with my private thoughts and feelings?
Has anyone ever repeated something of mine that was private?
How did that make me feel?
Have I ever repeated someone's private information? Why or why not?

~

Sharing the Load

If we have ever let a friend take the blame for something that we both participated in, then we weren't being a true friend. A real friend will share the load even if it means getting into trouble. Taking responsibility for our part in things is a noble, honest, and mature way to be. Letting a friend carry 'the load' alone is petty and selfish. We need to be the kind of friend that we want in our lives. A friend who is willing to share the load.

~

Have I ever let a friend take the blame for me? Why or why not?
Which of my friends would share the load?

~

Chapter 14: *Love*

It is a Gift

Love is a gift, a precious gift. And just like anything that's precious, it should be handled with care. The love we feel for our friends and family comes quite naturally. We may find ourselves experiencing feelings of romantic love that are as scary as they are exciting. Just know that this particular kind of love may be a little harder to handle, but should be cherished all the same. One of the most important kinds of love however, is the love we have for ourselves. Treating ourselves with respect and dignity will have a profound impact on our lives. Today and always … give ourselves the gift of love.

~

How do I treat myself with love?
What makes love such a special gift?

~

Showing Love

Showing love is as important as feeling loved. Being available to help out is one way to show the people in our lives that we care. Helping others and pitching in feels good for the giver and the receiver. Of course it's more fun to watch TV, play outside, talk on the phone, and play video games, but offering our help without being asked is a good way to show our loved ones that we appreciate them. It means that we're willing to put their needs ahead of our wants.

~

What was the last thing I did to show love?
Who shows their love to me regularly?
What are some things I can do to help out?

~

Love Our Lives

Loving our lives is easier said than done. There are many different areas of our lives — school, family, friendships, and hobbies — it may be hard to balance every area. Especially when we get overwhelmed and things just aren't going as planned. Although there will definitely be days when we feel frustrated, we must just breathe … and be grateful. If we can remember to love our lives and treat the people in it with love, the tough days won't seem so bad … and we'll appreciate the good days so much more.

~

What do I love about my life?
What do I find frustrating about my life?
What area/areas of my life are 'out of balance'?

~

My Family

When it comes to family we need to be there for each other. But sometimes loving our family can be truly challenging. Maybe our parents are always on our case. Or our siblings do things to annoy us … on purpose. No matter what the situation is, they are still our family and the only one we have. We must do our best to love, respect, and accept them exactly the way they are. Hopefully, they do the same for us!

~

What do my parents do that 'bugs' me?
How do my siblings annoy me?
What's the most loving thing my family does for me?
What do I do for them?

~

My Parents are So Strict!

Being strict is one way parents express the love they feel for a child. It is the parents' responsibility to keep their children safe. And because our parents want what's best for us, they may give us strict rules to follow ... rules that we may not think are fair. Parents who love their kids will take the time to create rules. So the next time our parents are strict ... remember that even though we may not like it, it means they truly love us.

~

What are some 'strict' rules that my parents have?
When I don't follow the rules ... what happens?
What kind of parent do I think I'll be?

~

Time to Heal

When those we love are hurting, we hurt, too. We want to do all we can to help them feel better. We may want to defend them, or do something to take their minds off the pain. But some things just need time to heal. The best thing we can do for loved ones is to let them know that we are there for them if they need us and then let them heal in their own time.

~

When was the last time I needed 'time' to heal?
Who was the last person to let me know that he (she) cared?
How did she (he) help me get through it?

~

Tough Love

Can people love us too much? Sometimes they can help us too much. Learning to be responsible for ourselves is part of growing up. If we have someone who helps us do everything, it may be hard for us to learn to do things for ourselves. That's where tough love may be the healthier choice. When we are allowed to make our own mistakes and feel the pain of the outcome, we're much more likely to learn from the experiences. It may be hard for our loved ones to watch … (that's why it's called tough love) but we'll be stronger in the long run.

~

Who tries to help me all the time?
Whom have I tried to help?
When have I experienced 'tough love'?

~

CHAPTER 15: *Humility*

... is a Gift

When we let someone go first, or we do something nice for someone without telling anyone, or we go out of our way to help ... that's humility. It's a gift for us because it feels good to be kind to others without expecting anything in return. It's a gift for others, because they will know how much we care. Wow! What a great way to live our lives!

~

Why is it important not to expect praise for doing something nice?
Who are the people I'd like to help?
Who has helped me without asking for anything in return?

~

Being Responsible

We've all probably said something to a friend that we wish we hadn't. We may want to take it back, but unfortunately, that's not possible. Practicing humility means being responsible. Being responsible means apologizing right away. If we wait too long, especially when we know we were wrong, our ego may keep us from saying something. Ego and humility cannot co-exist. We all make mistakes, but apologizing for our behavior is one way to be responsible for our actions and practice humility.

~

Do I owe anyone an apology?
What would I like to say to that person?
Are there any other behaviors that I need to take responsibility for?

~

Being Happy for Others

We all have friends we envy a little. Trying to be happy for others can sometimes be difficult. But practicing humility means that we congratulate them anyway. We might have to fake it, but once we see their faces light up, we're sure to feel good about our actions. It's okay to let someone else shine.

~

Do I sometimes envy someone?
Why am I jealous of this person?
What can I do to change these feelings?

~

Apologizing

When is the right time to apologize? Whenever we were wrong. If we know that we hurt someone's feelings, we should apologize. If we misunderstood what someone was saying, we need to apologize. If we show up late for something, apologize. Saying a simple "I'm sorry" can help to right a wrong. Apologizing really takes very little effort; however, it does take an attitude of humility. And the real growth comes from changing and trying not to make the same mistakes again. It's surprising how much better we'll feel after apologizing.

~

Why does it take 'humility' to apologize?
Do I owe anyone an apology?
If given the opportunity, what would I say?

~

Don't Judge a Book by its Cover

When we meet others … do we decide to be friends based on their "outsides"? Their hair, clothes, or where they live? Or do we base our decision on their "insides"? Maybe they are friendly and funny. The most beautiful-looking people can be mean and hateful, just as the most average-looking people can be kind and loving. The real value of a person comes from within. Appreciating others based on their "insides" is about practicing humility.

~

Who have I judged based on his or her outsides?
Are the people in my life close to me because of my insides?

~

It's Okay to Ask for Help

Sometimes we might be afraid to ask for help. We think we will embarrass ourselves because we don't know something. We think we will look dumb and people will make fun of us. But when we ask questions, it shows that we want to learn. Remembering that no one knows everything will help us realize that it's okay to ask questions. We are practicing humility when we can admit that we don't know everything. It also shows that we are open and willing to learn. So remember, the only dumb question … is the one we don't ask!

~

What have I been afraid to ask questions about?
Who can help me in this area?
Why does it take humility to ask for help?

~

It's Okay To 'Just' Listen

We've all grown in many areas of our lives and we're learning new things all the time. Sometimes conversations about life can be so exciting that we can't wait to express ourselves. We might even cut someone off while they're talking because we think that we already know what they're going to say. When we talk more than we listen…we are robbing ourselves of the gift of getting to know more about other people. Learning the things that are important to others; their likes and dislikes, are a part of making the connection that allows a relationship to grow. If we can practice humility….and listen…really listen to what others have to say, we'll be amazed at the new and exciting things that will come our way.

~

Do I talk more than I listen? Why / Why not?
What's the last thing I learned about someone by just listening?

~

Chapter 16: *Life*

Make the Most Out of Life

To make the most of our lives, our lives must have meaning. Some people give their lives meaning by helping others. For others, meaning comes from doing something that they are passionate about. The point is … whatever we find meaningful should be included in our lives on a regular basis.

~

How would I define the word meaningful?
What did I do today that's meaningful?
What would I like to be doing to make the most of my life?

~

The "Blahs"

As we grow older, we begin to understand that every day is not going to be perfect. Some days may be exciting, some days may be emotional, some days may be calm and some days are just plain blah. The blah days may be the hardest to get through because they're dull and may be a little depressing. But the truth is … blah days are a part of life. Just like the exciting times pass … so will the blahs.

~

What happened that last time I had a 'blah' day?
What can I do the next time I have a 'blah' day?

~

Nurturing Our Gift

Every person has the capacity to be great at something. We must look inside ourselves and figure out what we like to do that we are also good at. Then we must take the time to 'nurture' our gift so that we will be great at it. At the very least, we will build some self-esteem … but hopefully, we will be able to use our gift to help others.

~

What are my gifts? How can I nurture them?

~

Every Day is a Good Day

If we wake up in the morning with a purpose … it's a good day. If we have family and friends who love us … it's a good day. Even if we lose something important, have an argument with a friend, or ruin our favorite shirt … it can still be a good day. People often have bad moments, but rarely bad days. When something doesn't go our way, it doesn't have to ruin our day. We can use these experiences to our advantage, learn the lesson, and move on. If we have any reason at all to smile, then it's a good day.

~

How do I react when things don't go my way?
When was the last time I had a "bad" day?
What do I have to smile about today?

~

The Finish Line

Some people live their lives as if they are racing toward the finish line to get a prize. That may be how we win a race, but it may not be the best way to live life. Life is not a race to the finish line. Being ambitious is always a valuable asset, but when we race to the finish line, we may be running so fast we miss all of the beauty that life has to offer. The joy is in the journey … not in winning the race.

~

Do I race through my life? Why?
Am I always 'competing' with someone? Who?

~

Rainy Days

Some people wish that every day would be sunny and it would never rain. Some people think that life should always go as planned and that bad things shouldn't happen. But that's not reality. Life just happens and what happens isn't personal — it just is. There's a perfect balance to the world that is totally out of our control. For every left there is a right and for every good there is a bad … and so on. If we didn't have rainy days, we wouldn't appreciate the sunny ones.

~

Why is it unrealistic for things to always be a certain way?
What can I do to change my attitude about 'rainy' days?

~

Balance Beam

Life can be a lot like a balance beam. Remembering to give equal time and attention to the important things in our lives will help us stay balanced. Obviously, some things are going to be a lot easier to give our attention to than others. That's when our determination and commitment will speak for itself. When something unexpected gets thrown our way, we will be able to remain balanced if we are determined to stay focused on the big picture and use discipline so we don't get off track. This will ensure that no area of our lives gets left behind.

~

Why is a balanced life important?
Do I know someone who has a balanced life?
What do I need to do to put more balance in my life?

~

CHAPTER 17: *Trust*

Losing Trust from Our Family

Losing the trust of our family can be a hard and painful lesson to learn. Gaining their trust back is usually something that has to happen over time … not overnight. If we have broken their trust by lying or stealing or by doing something that got us in trouble, it's normal for them to feel betrayed and be cautious now about believing what we say. Be patient with them. When someone is hurt, it can take time for that wound to heal.

~

Who are the family members I trust?
Who are the family members that trust me?
When was the last time I lost someone's trust?

~

Trusting Our Friends

Trust is … relying on the honesty of another person. Trusting our friends is something that most people want to do. It feels natural. Before someone lets us down … trusting people may seem easy. Once our trust has been broken, we will realize that not everyone is trustworthy. Even our closest friends are human. And humans make mistakes. That's why trust is earned instead of given. As our friendships grow, and we observe people, we will be much better equipped to decide who is worthy of our trust.

~

Who are the friends I trust? Why do I trust them?

~

Am I Trustworthy?

Keeping someone else's trust is vital in a friendship. When someone tells us something and asks us to not tell anyone, they are counting on us to be trustworthy. As long as their secret isn't going to hurt anyone, it is not okay to repeat it … even if we're sure they'll never find out. We cannot expect others to be trustworthy if we can't be trusted ourselves.

~

Have I ever told someone else's secret? Why did I tell?

~

A Daily Decision

For some people, being trustworthy comes naturally. They wouldn't think of lying. The rest of us have to work at it. Being a trustworthy person is a decision that we make. We decide to be honest. And each day we can make that decision all over again. Just because we may have told a lie before doesn't mean we have to do it again. Each day is a new opportunity to be a person others can trust.

~

Why is it important to be a trustworthy person?
Have I ever gone to someone and admitted that I lied?
Why or why not?

~

Trusting Ourselves

The person we should be able to trust most in life is ourselves. We want to be able to trust ourselves to make healthy decisions and choices. Sometimes this will be easier than other times. When we're not quite sure what the healthy choice is … we need to ask someone that we trust to help us. A big part of trusting ourselves is knowing that we've surrounded ourselves with people who will tell us the truth.

~

Why is it important that I trust myself?
When was the last time I didn't trust myself?

~

Keeping Our Word

Our word is our bond. This means that if we say we're going to do something, people can trust that we'll do it. But if we're a person who simply says we're going to do something … then doesn't follow through, people will view us as unreliable and flaky. If we want to be people who keep our word, we can start by paying attention to the things we promise. We should only make promises we can actually keep, want to keep, and intend to keep. When we are people who keep our word, people will trust what we say.

~

Who are the reliable people in my life?
Who are the people that know they can count on me?

~

Storytelling

People want to trust what we tell them. And our reputations will depend on our past. If we have a history of telling the truth, then people will believe what we tell them. When we tell stories, we must make sure to tell the whole story the way it really happened. When we embellish to jazz it up, or leave out certain details to create a better effect, we are actually telling a lie. And even though it may seem harmless, eventually it will catch up with us and we'll regret it. If we want people to trust us … then we have to tell the truth.

~

Have I ever embellished a story to 'jazz it up'? Why?
Why is it important to tell the story the way it actually happens?

~

Chapter 18: *Anger*

Understanding People

Someone may have borrowed something of ours that was important and ruined it, or maybe even borrowed it without our permission. He or she may even have acted like it was no big deal after we let him know how much it bothered us. Sometimes people won't take care of our things like we will. This can make us really angry. We get mad because we feel mistreated and unimportant. We need to remember that not everyone is good at apologies and some people are just plain stubborn. Sometimes we just have to let go of the idea that we're owed something. Trying to understand people when we feel angry is hard to do but necessary.

~

How do I handle my anger when I feel mistreated?
Have I ever mistreated someone's belongings?

~

Feeling Hurt

That's not fair! We've probably all said that to our parents, our teachers, or our friends. When something seems unfair, we feel hurt. We might even tell ourselves that things are always unfair. But that's not the truth. It just feels that way while we're hurt and upset. We should take some quiet time to think about things. Usually after some time passes, we can accept whatever has happened and move on.

~

What happened to me recently that felt unfair?
How did I deal with my feelings?
Why does it help to take some quiet time to think about things?

~

Reacting

It's common for people to get angry and react. Some of us have said horrible things to the people we really love in the heat of the moment. When we let our feelings get the best of us we sometimes say things that we really don't mean. When we react to our feelings too quickly, we are not only hurting others … we are also hurting ourselves. When we take the time to calm down and maybe even get someone else's opinion, we can usually handle the situation without causing more harm. This would be 'acting' instead of 'reacting.'

~

When's the last time I caused harm by reacting instead of acting?
Did I regret my reaction?
What could I have done differently?

~

Taking Care of Ourselves

We may have a friend or relative who always seems to be picking on us. Some people actually try to make us angry. This can be difficult to deal with. Sometimes all we can do is stay quiet and clench our teeth until they leave us alone. Speaking up for ourselves can be really scary. But it's one of the best things we can learn to do. Sometimes a simple "please stop" can makes us feel stronger. Even if the person doesn't stop, we feel better knowing that we took care of ourselves.

~

Have I tried to speak up for myself?
Have I ever bullied someone?

~

Everyone Makes Mistakes

If we sometimes find ourselves judging our parents more harshly than everyone else, that's pretty common. Most of us have very high expectations of our parents. And as we grow up and mature, we realize that parents are just people, too. They will make mistakes just like everyone else. And just as we are learning to deal with our anger toward others, remember 'others' includes our parents.

~

What's the last thing my parents did that made me angry?
Have I forgiven them?

~

Getting Angry

Anger is a normal human emotion. Some people throw tantrums when they get angry … slam doors, yell at people, call people names, use profanity, and even cry. Believe it or not, these are reasonably normal reactions. If we find ourselves wanting to hurt someone or ourselves when we get angry, we should find someone to talk to about it. Causing ourselves or someone else physical harm is unacceptable … even if we're angry. Especially when we're angry. Things can quickly get out of control if our anger turns to rage. Life isn't always fair, and bad things do happen. Allowing ourselves to feel angry is healthy … but letting it turn to rage is completely destructive.

~

Has my anger ever turned into rage?
How far did it go?
Who can I go to for help when I get angry?

~

Having a Bad Day

Do we know how to have a bad day? It's important. We all have bad days and we don't want to fall apart just because our day didn't go as planned. Once we've acknowledged our disappointment, we can start our day over. Even if we don't think things will get any better, it's healthy to make a new plan, put it into action and hopefully our attitude will change. Be constructive with our anger. It will help.

~

What happened the last time I had a bad day?
How did I pull myself out of it?
How can I start my day over?

~

CHAPTER 19: *Choices*

We Get to Decide

When someone is encouraging us to do something that just doesn't seem right, it's okay to take a moment to look at our choices. Sometimes taking a minute to think can be the difference between a good decision and a bad decision. As we begin to take responsibility for our own lives, it will be our choices that determine what's important to us. We can decide for ourselves or have others decide for us.

~

Why is it important to stand by our own choices?
When is it okay to let someone else make the decisions?

~

Making Decisions

As responsible young adults, we can obviously think for ourselves. But sometimes we might not know what to do. Making decisions can be tough. When we are struggling with a decision, it's okay to ask for help. This is when running things past our family members or a counselor is a good choice. Talk to others. They might be able to offer sound advice.

~

When do I struggle the most with making decisions?
What area of my life is the easiest to make decisions about?
Who can help me make healthy choices?

~

Keep Calm

Keep a cool head. Don't panic. Stay calm and count to ten. We use this advice when we become angry, scared, or have an emergency. It will help us make better decisions during a time when we might be too excited to think straight or choose carefully. The whole point is to remain level-headed. This way, we can think clearly on how to solve the problem and help others in the process.

~

When was the last time I panicked? What happened?
How would it have been different ... if I would've been calm?

~

Friendships

No one should have to choose between friends. Good friends will not put demands on a relationship. They will not expect us to put them first. They will respect our priorities. Friendships should be easy. But first we must choose healthy people to be our friends.

~

Who are my friends that make friendship easy?
What makes a healthy friendship?

~

Safety and Common Sense

If something doesn't feel right in our "gut" … we should not ignore it. When confronted with a choice that involves our safety, we might want to use some common sense. That is, listen to our instincts. Our "gut feeling" will remind us about all we have learned and been taught in our lifetimes. These are the lessons that will help us to make healthy, safe choices. There are times in our lives to take risks, but not when it involves our safety. Taking risks should be for choosing a new outfit.

~

When have I chosen not to listen to my gut instincts?
What were the results of my decision?

~

Jack of All Trades

There is so much to do in this world it is impossible to do everything. So we have to choose. The saying, "Jack of all trades … master of none," means we may know how to do a lot of things, but can we do any of them well? There's nothing wrong with exploring different options, but if it matters to us to be good at something, then we should focus on learning how to do one thing really well.

~

What am I interested in learning to do well?
Who can help me?

~

Choosing Wisely

When we know who we are … our choices will reflect our unique qualities. Everything from our choice of friends to our choice of music is an expression of us. If we find ourselves making choices based on being liked or being popular, people will not know who we really are … and neither will we. Checking our motives will help us stay true to ourselves in our choices. When we embrace who we really are, others will do the same.

~

What is my favorite kind of music, or my favorite movie?
Who is my closest friend?
What's my favorite hobby? Where do I like to shop?
Why are these my choices?

~

CHAPTER 20: *All about Me*

Changing

As we get older, change is inevitable. These changes can be awkward and uncomfortable. Some of us feel like our bodies have outgrown our emotions, and others may feel the exact opposite. Either way, rest assured that eventually it will all balance out. Everyone goes through these changes. And just about everyone feels like an alien at some point. It's all perfectly normal.

~

What changes have I noticed physically?
What's changed about me emotionally?

~

Style

We can be just like our friends and all dress the same or we can be unique and have our own personal style, especially when we express our personalities. With all the different styles to choose from … we can dress appropriately, trendy, and still have fun being ourselves. We can find our own styles and have fun with it.

~

What does 'style' mean to me?
How would I describe my style? Sporty? Frilly? Casual? Why?

~

Goals

We've all had fantasies about being rich and famous someday. And even though most of us won't be ... setting goals is important. It gives us hope for the future. If we can see ourselves doing something, then it's possible to achieve. We need to find out what we're passionate about and then set some goals for ourselves.

~

What am I passionate about?
What are my goals for the future?
What can I do today to move toward those goals?

~

Be Grateful

Sometimes it seems like everything goes wrong. We can feel sorry for ourselves or we can not let it bother us. A great way to do this is to find something in our lives to be grateful for or think of some way to help someone else. That's the easiest way to turn our day around. The power to forget what went wrong comes from inside of us.

~

What things am I grateful for today? Who can I help today?

~

Surrender

It's never comfortable arguing with someone. Some of us become desperate to be right. And as our desperation grows, the things we say can become more and more extreme. We may think that if we win the fight, we'll feel better. But this is rarely true. Once a disagreement turns into an argument, there are no winners … only hurt feelings. The solution to ending an argument is to surrender. That means … stop, breathe, walk away, and let go of the idea of winning. Once we're calm, we can usually resolve the situation easily. But surrender has to come first.

~

When was the last time I had an argument with someone?
How did it get resolved?

~

Finding Balance

Life can be very busy. We all have responsibilities. Homework, practice, chores, and maybe even a job. It's easy to get overwhelmed with all the things we have to get done. Taking the time to laugh with a friend, work on a hobby, or just have a little fun, is as important as all of our other responsibilities. In fact, when we lighten up from time to time, we may not feel as overwhelmed … because we'll have balance.

~

What happens when I feel overwhelmed?
What does balance mean to me?
What can I do to 'lighten up' today?

~

Self-esteem

Self-esteem is vital to a healthy, happy life. And discipline is a key component of gaining self-esteem. We need to feel good about ourselves. If we want to build self-esteem … then we must do esteem-able things. Take care of ourselves, eat healthy, get enough rest, be honest, follow through with our commitments, help others, and don't give up. It sounds like a lot … and it is … but when we do these things to the best of our ability every day, we will build a wealth of self-esteem. And when we have self-esteem, it shows and we're bound to attract people who have self-esteem as well. With that kind of support around … we can achieve anything!

~

What does it mean to have self-esteem?
Do I have self-esteem?
What can I do to work on my self-esteem?

~

CHAPTER 21: *Disappointments*

Tough Times

Tough times are a part of life and they happen to everyone. The way we handle ourselves during tough times is important. Each experience in life gives us a lesson. If we choose to handle our disappointments with maturity, then we will benefit from the lesson. If we react to our disappointments with immaturity … then we are probably going to have to learn that lesson again. A true sign of growth is when we can learn from our tough times.

~

How do I handle disappointments?
What does it mean to handle tough times with maturity?
What's the last lesson I learned from a disappointment?

~

Expectations

When we're expecting something and it doesn't happen … it hurts. When we put expectations on anything in life, it can be dangerous. Expectations are a set-up for future disappointments. It's okay to hope for things; however, hoping and expecting are two very different things. We hope for things with no expectation of them happening. When we expect things, we've already decided that it's going to happen. So when it doesn't … we get disappointed. Hoping for the best and preparing for the worst will keep us from getting hurt in the end.

~

What are the things I hope for today?
What are the things I am expecting to happen?
How can I avoid future disappointments?

~

Wanting

Sometimes we want something so badly that we can't stop thinking about it. We become so fixed on an idea that we may actually believe we won't be okay without it. But this is rarely the truth. We probably have a lot to be grateful for and could live the rest of our lives perfectly happy without whatever it is. If we stay focused on what we do have instead of what we don't have … the gifts in life will be a pleasant surprise. And the desperate wanting will disappear.

~

What's the last thing I really wanted?
What am I'm grateful for?

~

Grieving

When someone we love is suddenly gone, it hurts. It could be a grandparent who dies or a best friend who moves away. It could be a pet who is gone. It hurts and we feel lonely. We may find ourselves crying about it. This is also normal. After some time passes, we may notice that we don't hurt as much. And after more time passes, we may not hurt at all. We just smile when we think of them. Why? Because time heals, but the amount of time varies. The grieving process is different for everyone. We need to let ours take its natural course. There's no wrong way to grieve.

~

When was the last time I grieved? How did I grieve?

~

No, No, No!

Sometimes it seems like the answer to everything we ask for is … no! It's hard to hear no over and over again. But we won't hear it as much if we learn to choose between the things we really want and the stuff we see on TV or hear about from our friends. Choosing what we really want comes with maturity. We begin to understand that if we get everything we ask for … the things that are truly special won't have the same meaning.

~

Why do I think my parents tell me no?
What would happen if they always said yes?

~

Friendships

Sometimes friends can let us down. It happens in almost every friendship at least once. There are other times when we may find our friendships changing. Maybe we're not spending as much time together or it seems that we just don't have very much in common anymore. This can be disappointing and sometimes hard to accept. Especially when we've been really close to someone. Feeling the pain is part of the process of change. Friendships change and people outgrow each other. But that doesn't have to be a bad thing. Maybe it is just time to move on. Maybe we'll try some new things and make new friends. Looking at things as an opportunity instead of a pitfall will help us get through the disappointment much quicker.

~

Who are my best friends?
Have any of my friendships ever changed? Why?
How did I get through it?

~

A Learning Experience

Life won't always go the way we hope it will. Unexpected things happen all the time that disappoint us. When something is disappointing we may label it as "bad" or "unfair". But we don't have to label every disappointing experience. We can do away with the label and change our point of view. If we can look at our disappointments and think about what we could have done differently, what we'll do differently next time or what this experience has taught us…we have now turned our disappointment into a tool for learning.

~

What was the last thing that I was disappointed by?
What can I learn from this experience?

~

CHAPTER 22: *Courage*

Changing Our Minds

We've all probably said we would do something and then later decided to change our minds. Maybe we decided that something wasn't such a good idea after all … but now we need to tell our friends and that can sometimes be hard. There is a lot of power in being able to change our minds and not feel bad about it. But it can take courage. Decisions like this can be difficult but the great thing about being an individual is that we get to decide to change our minds and be true to ourselves instead of trying to be liked.

~

How is changing my mind different than keeping my word?
What's the last thing I changed my mind about?

~

Courage and Fears

Fear is focusing on negative thoughts. And everyone is afraid of something. When we have fears and we walk through them … we are being courageous. Courage comes from facing our fears. We can feel afraid and practice courage at the same time. No matter what it is we fear we can replace the negative thoughts with positive reinforcements by telling ourselves … "I'm okay … I can do this." Eventually, that fear will lose its power over us.

~

What am I afraid of?
What are the negative thoughts that taunt me about this fear?
How can I overcome this fear and face it?

~

Mean People

We all know at least one "mean" person. Maybe it's someone we go to school with or someone from our neighborhood. It's hard to handle being around a bully. We may want to be mean back or at least talk about that person when he's not around. But neither one of these things will change the situation. Nor are they the right things to do. What should we do instead? Walking away is always a good option. Walking away is a very powerful response and there isn't much anyone can do about it. It shows that we've had enough and we're taking care of ourselves.

~

How do I handle "mean" people?
Have I ever been the "mean" person?

~

New Relationships

When we watch small kids play together, we see them play so simply; no introduction needed … they just play with each other. Unfortunately, that begins to change as we get older. We become more self-conscious and that can stop us from following our true nature. It may take more courage today to make friends than when we were five, but it's probably not as hard as we make it out to be. A simple "hello" is all we need to get started. Chances are the other person is just as nervous as we are.

~

Who would I like to make friends with?
What have I done to start the relationship?
What am I afraid of?

~

Instinct

What is instinct? It is a powerful feeling, often with common sense. We may be afraid to face our fears, but there may also be a very good reason for our fears. Maybe we should be afraid. When we're faced with a potentially dangerous situation … it's important to listen to our instincts and use our common sense. Better safe than sorry. We can learn to decide if our fears are legitimate or unreasonable.

~

How have I used common sense lately?
What are some legitimate things to fear?

~

Just Say No!

It takes courage to say no to our friends and take the risk of not being liked. Deciding what to do should come from doing what is right, not from wanting to fit in. We all want to belong somewhere and be liked. But that shouldn't be more important than doing the next right thing. When we care enough about ourselves to say "no" to harmful temptations, it shows confidence and comfort in our own skin. What we do today is the beginning of who we will be tomorrow. Do we have the courage to say no regardless of what others may think?

~

What have I been tempted to do that was harmful?
Am I afraid of not fitting in? Why or why not?

~

Stand for Something

There are times in life when we need to mind our own business and then there are times that we need to take a stand. Knowing the difference is the tricky part. If someone is being hurt, then we need to tell. Period. If our friends are in an argument … it's not our business. If a friend is gossiping about another friend, not participating is always an option. All of these scenarios require taking a stand one way or another. In every situation in life, we need to think first … then practice the courage to do the right thing. Choosing our battles is as important as how we decide to handle them once we choose.

~

Why should we choose our battles carefully?
Why is it important to take a stand?
How do I know when to stay out of it?

~

CHAPTER 23: *Ego*

The Good

Ego is the part of our thinking that helps us figure out our own sense of importance and self-worth. It also dictates how we react to the outside world. When we're getting ready for school in the morning, we'll probably do our best to look good. Partly because it feels better when we look good … but the other reason is because our ego wants other people to see that we look good. It is our ego that looks to the outside world for approval. Sometimes the positive reactions we get from others helps us build self-esteem.

~

Who do I look to for approval?
What does my ego tell me about myself?

~

The Bad

People who think very highly of themselves are often called egomaniacs. They may have an attitude that says … "you're lucky to be in my presence!" Their attitude makes them unattractive both inside and out. There's a big difference between having a healthy self-esteem and being self-absorbed.

~

Do I think too highly of myself?
How can I exhibit a healthy self-esteem without being self-absorbed?

~

The Ugly

Another part of our ego is truly destructive: when we aren't humble enough to apologize for something or admit when we're wrong. This is one of the quickest ways to destroy a friendship. No one wants to be in a relationship with someone who always has to be right.

~

When was the last time I couldn't admit I was wrong?
What stopped me from being humble?
How did it affect my relationships?

~

Gratitude

Sometimes it may seem like everyone has more than we do. Someone at school may have more expensive clothes, or someone we know may have all of the latest video games. If we keep looking for people who have more than we have, we will always find someone. But guess what? There's someone who looks at us the same way. Some people have more … some people have less. It's the way of the world. When we allow our egos to get in the way of our gratitude, it's easy to forget what really matters.

~

What matters most in my life?
Why is it important to be grateful for what I have?

~

Attention-seeking Behavior

Some people go out of their way to keep the focus on them. They may be loud and dramatic just to keep others' attention. They use the attention of others to feed their egos for the purpose of feeling important. What they're really looking for is self-esteem. But self-esteem comes from doing "esteem-able" things, not from making a spectacle of oneself. If we are helpful, respectful, and kind to people we will feel important … and it will be for the right reasons.

~

What have I done to build self-esteem?
When have I acted in attention-seeking behavior?
Why do I need to feel important?

~

It's Not My Fault

When things go wrong in a friendship, sometimes it is easier to place blame on the other person than it is to look at our part. If it's not our fault, then we won't have to change anything. But if nothing changes … then nothing changes. There is a tremendous amount of maturity and growth that comes from putting our egos aside, looking at our behavior, and taking responsibility for our part. In the big picture … it doesn't matter who is at fault. All that matters is making the appropriate changes so we can move forward.

~

When was the last time I placed blame on someone?
How did I resolve the situation?

~

Speaking From the Heart

Speaking from the heart is crucial to making relationships work. When we remove our egos and speak from our hearts, we can change the course of a conversation. If someone says he doesn't like us, our ego-based response might be, "Well, I don't like you, either!" That's a natural reaction when our feelings are hurt and we want to protect ourselves. But if we speak from our heart … we might say something like, "I'm sorry you feel that way." The ego-based response might feel better at first, but when we speak from our hearts, we have a much better chance of resolving the conflict.

~

Why is it better to speak from my heart?
When am I able to speak from my heart?
What would keep me from speaking from my heart?

~

CHAPTER 24: *Awareness*

Diversity

Some people try really hard to simply blend in. Others wouldn't be able to blend in even if they tried. They just stand out. As we grow up and mature … we can appreciate our diversity. That means we are aware of all the things that make us different from other people. We are all just a bit different on the outside. As we venture out into the world, we can embrace and be grateful for the diversity in society. The world would be terribly dull without it.

~

Why is diversity a good thing?
What makes me completely different from anyone else?

~

Be Aware of Our Surroundings

When we go outside … we need to be aware of our surroundings. When we're hanging out with friends, listening to music, or texting on the phone … it's easy to forget to stay aware of what's around us. However, when we are away from the safety of our homes, that's the most important time to be aware. If there's something we need to take action on, we should know how to get help right away. Awareness doesn't mean that we should walk around afraid and suspicious all the time. It just means that we understand the importance of taking care of ourselves.

~

How can I be more aware of my surroundings?
Why is it important to be aware?
Do I know how and where to get help if there's an emergency?

~

Helping Others in Our Community

No matter where we come from, the idea of helping others is probably something we have heard many times in our lives. Some people will say it's the reason we are here … to help others. One person can make a difference in the world. If we think of people in our lives that we admire and why … it's probably because they make a difference. And helping others in our community is how we can start.

~

What can I do to help people in my community?
Who has helped me?

~

Go Green!

There is an awareness growing among us to take responsibility to do our part to help save this planet. We all need to consider whether we are a part of the problem or the solution. When we litter, leave the lights on or the water running, or throw away things that we could recycle … that contributes to the problem. When we turn off the lights, recycle plastic and paper, and walk as far away as necessary to find a trash can, we're in the solution. If we are aware that no matter how small our contribution is … we are affecting the big picture.

~

Why is it important to help the planet in any way possible?
What have I done that's a part of the problem?
What am I willing to change to be a part of the solution?

~

No Means No

We all like getting our own way. And no one is wild about hearing "no" for the answer. However, as bad as 'no' sounds … it's even harder when we refuse to accept it as the answer. Badgering is not cool. It's called manipulation. When we manipulate someone to get our way, by begging, pleading, or threatening them, they will lose respect for us and eventually stop trusting us. No means no … and it's okay to let it go at that and move on.

~

Have I ever badgered anyone after being told no?
Why did I continue after hearing no?

~

When to Seek Help

Some people let things get way too far out of control before they'll ask for help. Some people might not even be aware that there's a problem. Knowing when to ask for help is important. If we're not sure about something, or it just doesn't feel right … we need to ask for help! We should never be afraid to use the support of the people in our lives. Our parents, friends, teachers, and counselors want us to succeed.

~

How do I know when something has turned into a problem?
What are my fears about asking for help?

~

Feelings

Being aware of our feelings can help us stay grounded. Sometimes our feelings can have us all over the place. Happy, sad, excited, afraid, and insecure are all very powerful feelings. And sometimes it seems like they last forever. But they don't. All feelings change over time. So when we react impulsively to our feelings, we may make decisions that we'll regret later. It's important to remember that the best decisions are made when we're not caught up in the feeling.

~

How do I identify what I am feeling?
Which feelings are the hardest for me to feel?
Why should I wait until a feeling passes before I react?

~

Chapter 25: *Priorities*

Knowing Ours

We should always be clear on our priorities. The basics like food and shelter are important to everyone. But what comes next in our lives? Some people put time with their families first, while others think that friends or school are more important. There are no right or wrong answers … we just need to know what our priorities are. When we know what's important to us … it's easier to stay on track.

~

What's at the top of my list of priorities? Why?
What's at the bottom? Why?

~

Wants and Needs

It's easy to get our priorities mixed up between our needs and our wants. They can sometimes feel like the same things … but they are not. Our need for clothing and shelter is obviously a very basic need. But wanting the latest outfit from the mall or to live in a big fancy house is not a priority. There is nothing wrong with wanting nice things, but if getting our "wants" is more important than being grateful that our needs are met, then it's time to straighten out our priorities.

~

What are the things I want today?
What are the things I need?
What is the difference between my wants and my needs?

~

Getting a Good Start

Getting a good start to our day should be a priority. Believe it or not … being a morning person has more to do with what we did the night before than whether we like or dislike mornings. When we know we have an early class or an important event to attend in the morning, we'll have a much better attitude about it if we take care of ourselves the night before. So before we watch a marathon of our favorite show … or eat a bag of potato chips at midnight, we need to think about what we have to do tomorrow and how we want to feel. Maybe eating healthy and getting a good night's rest will help us have a better day tomorrow.

~

What kind of mood do I wake up in?
Do I jump out of bed … or hit the snooze button on my alarm clock five times?
What time do I go to bed?
Would my day be better if I got a good start? Why or why not?

~

Personal Growth

Personal growth should always be on our list of priorities. Hopefully, there are things about us that we are working on, trying to improve. Maybe we want to be a better friend, help around the house more, or focus on getting better grades. These are all things that if made a priority … would definitely impact our futures. The people we are today are not necessarily the people we will be tomorrow … as long as we are working on ourselves. Our personal growth, internally, is as important as any of our other priorities. We must make sure to put us on our list.

~

What does personal growth mean to me?
What areas of personal growth would I like to work on?

~

Look at the Big Picture

Having our priorities straight will give us a sense of direction … a road map to what is important to us. When we are planning our future, we want to remember our priorities. There will be times when we'll have to pick one thing over another based on its level of importance. Remembering our ultimate goal and looking at the "big picture" will help us with these decisions. Friendships and having fun should have a place on our list of priorities. But we must be responsible and honest with ourselves. If we know that we need study or practice for something instead of hanging out with our friends, we could easily talk ourselves into doing what feels better rather than doing what is better. This is when we have to remind ourselves of our priorities. Is hanging out with our friends going to help us achieve our goals? Will our friends be there to hang out another time? We already know the answers.

~

Do my friendships get in the way of my priorities?
Do I make excuses so that having fun is more of a priority than achieving my goals?
What do I want to achieve in the future?

~

Money

If we don't already have a job or earn money now, we probably will soon. And the thing about money is it needs respect. When we work hard for our money, we deserve to enjoy the freedom that comes with it. But if our priorities aren't straight, we could easily act irresponsibly and have nothing to show for it. Knowing how to manage money is like learning how to drive a car. When a person becomes old enough to drive a car … he slowly learns the rules of the road before he's given a license to drive. Money should be handled the same way. There are some basic rules that we will need to be taught. Learning about earning, saving, and spending money is one of the most valuable lessons that we'll ever learn. If we make it a priority, we save ourselves the stress of doing it the hard way.

~

How do I earn money today?
What do I like to spend my money on?
Who can I ask to teach me about the rules that come with having money?

~

Pay ATTENTION!

Have you ever been listening to someone and realized that you weren't paying attention to anything they said? This can be a common issue for many of us. We may have missed out on some valuable information simply because we were daydreaming instead of paying attention. Turning our thoughts off and paying attention should be a priority. It can be the difference between getting a "C" on a test…or getting an "A". Paying attention can determine how well we will be able to do things for ourselves…when it's time. There are so many things to learn as we grow up. We'll need to pay attention along the way to ensure our success.

~

Is paying attention a priority to me? Why / Why not?
How well do I pay attention?

~

CHAPTER 26: *Changes*

The New Me

As our bodies start to change, it may feel awkward. Our thoughts about our bodies will also start to change. These changes are normal. We may feel like an alien sometimes and a movie star at other times; it's all okay. There are no topics that are off limits while we're going through this. So remember to let our friends and family in on how we're feeling so we don't have to do it alone. Everyone has to experience these changes.

~

What are the changes I've noticed about my body lately?
How have my thoughts about my body changed lately?
What am I afraid to talk about?

~

Screen Time

Screen time of any kind can be very entertaining, relaxing, and it's fun. It's so much fun that sometimes it's easy to have too much of it. There is more to life than screen time. It might be a good idea to take a look at our daily routine and make sure that we have a balance between our family, friends, school, and "me" time. As we are growing and changing, we need to be sure our focus is balanced.

~

How have I changed in the past year?
How much time do I spend watching TV, texting or on social media?
Do I feel 'balanced' in my life? Why or why not?

~

Keep it Interesting

Some things come so easily that they begin to require little or no effort. Putting in effort keeps us stimulated. Even our favorite subject at school can become boring if it's too easy for too long. This is when we need to "step it up." Challenge ourselves. How? If it's a subject at school, we can ask the teacher for more advanced work. If it's a sport or hobby, we can try to participate in it with more experienced people. When we change the level of difficulty … we also change the level of interest.

~

In what areas do I need more of a challenge?
What can I do to keep it interesting?

~

Feelings

When we realize for the first time that someone we are friends with, we now like in a different way, it can be the best and the worst feeling. We may want to panic and run … or try really hard to control everything. But we really don't have to do anything at all. And nothing in the relationship has to change if we don't want it to. Liking someone … really liking someone … is a natural part of life and things tend to take their own natural course when we let them. So all we're responsible for is feeling our feelings. Everything else will work itself out.

~

Who do I like as more than a friend?
Do I think this person feels the same way about me?
Who can I talk to about these feelings?

~

Growing Up

As we continue to change and grow into young adulthood, we'll probably rely less on our parents and more on ourselves for decisions. Although it's healthy and perfectly normal to become more independent, it's important to remember that there's no harm in running things past our parents. If we start to believe that we no longer need anyone's input in our lives and can make all of our own decisions, it may cause friction with our family and lead to some painful mistakes. It's okay to take our time growing up and be patient with our family as they adjust to the new independent us.

~

What decisions can I now make for myself?
What areas do I still need input from my family?

~

Opening Up

Part of growing up … is opening up. It's really important to find a balance between our independence and seeking input from others. When we open up and talk to the people we trust about the changes we're going through, then listen to what they have to say with an open mind, we may receive some great advice that we would not have known about on our own. The more information we have before making a decision, the healthier the decision will be.

~

Who are the people I trust to open up to?
Who are the people that open up to me?
Why is it a good idea to get input before making decisions?

~

Life

Life rarely stays the same for too long. Every year a new grade level. New activities, learning to drive; maybe there are even changes in our family. We all go through life changes. Sometimes they're good and sometimes they hurt. But we have a choice in how we react to our life changes. We can accept changes as they come, learning to adapt to our new surroundings. Or we can fight them and end up doing more damage than is necessary. The choice is ours.

~

How would I describe the changes that have taken place in my life?
How have I reacted to these changes?
Do I "go with the flow"? Why or why not?

~

CHAPTER 27: *Feelings*

Butterflies

Ever had 'butterflies'? It's that feeling of adrenalin that jumps out at us and grabs us by surprise when we're about to do or see something exciting, hear something exciting or upsetting. A nervousness in our stomach is our body's "red flag." It's telling us to proceed with caution because whatever we heard, saw or are about to do has the potential to be very powerful. When our bodies warn us with butterflies … we should not ignore this feeling. We must examine where this feeling came from … then decide what to do about it.

~

When was the last time I had butterflies in my stomach?
Why is it important to find out why I had this feeling?

~

Sadness

Sometimes we feel sad for no reason at all. A lot of people do. Sometimes when sad feelings hit us, all we can do is feel them. We don't have to be "mean" to people because we feel sad. We don't have to "hide" from people because we feel sad. We can go on with our day and do everything we're supposed to do while we feel sad, because no matter how we feel right now we won't feel that way forever.

~

Why is sadness such a hard feeling to get through?
When was the last time I felt sad?
What are some other feelings that I have difficulty with?

~

Anger

We don't always know the difference between hurt feelings and angry feelings. That's because hurt feelings are usually what angry feelings are covering up. Anger is our first reaction ... but when we get quiet and calm down long enough, we'll probably find that the truth is our feelings were hurt. Once we get to the root of our feelings, we can deal with the real problem instead of covering them up with anger.

~

What do I feel angry about?
Why do I feel angry about it?

~

Fear

When we are "afraid" of something, it can paralyze us, because fear is one of the most powerful feelings. Keeping "fear" in perspective is a hard thing to do. Sometimes we can be "afraid" of things that will never happen. Staying in the moment is a good way to conquer that feeling. We have to simply keep telling ourselves ... "I'm okay right now ... I'm okay," and before we know it, the feeling will pass.

~

What am I most afraid of?
Why do I have this fear?
Who can help me get through it?

~

Accepting Others

Some people are friendly and some people aren't. Some people share and some people don't. No one is always one way or the other. When someone hurts our feelings by not sharing or by not being friendly, we have to cut them some slack. After all, we don't always share. Sometimes we don't feel like being friendly. Keeping this in mind will help us understand others and try not to take things so personally.

~

When have I not been friendly?
How do I think others feel why I'm not friendly?
What do I do to stop being unfriendly?

~

Making Choices

Making healthy choices requires a sound mind with accurate information. Making choices based on feelings is not such a healthy idea. Why? Because we're most likely to be the least logical when we're caught up in an emotion. This includes "peer pressure." If we decide to do something because we feel afraid of what someone might think … this is a prime example of making an unhealthy choice based on a feeling. The results can be very painful and we'll end up regretting our decision. The healthiest decisions are made when we've gathered all the information first and no emotion is attached.

~

What's the last choice I made that I regret?
What's the last healthy choice I made?
Why do I worry about what people will think?

~

Following Our Hearts

Following our hearts is about doing what we love, about doing something that moves us. As we have different experiences in life, we will hopefully come across something that we feel passionate about. Once we know what that special something is for us, we'll want to find a way to incorporate that into our lives. Whether it's working with animals, children, playing an instrument or studying medicine, we can't stop searching for the thing that makes us feel good about who we are. Life can be that much better if we are spending it doing something that we feel passionate about.

~

What am I passionate about?
How can I pursue this passion?
Who do I share this passion with?

~

CHAPTER 28: *Growing Up*

Helping Out

When we were little ... our parents would praise us as "good little helpers." Even when they had to re-do whatever it was that we did. Now that we are older the question is ... does our help really help or does someone have to go behind us and re-do it? We might be amazed how much of a difference we could really make by helping out if we truly make an effort, take our time, and follow through. We could probably run the household if we had to. We have been watching all of these years. We know exactly how to do it all. A sure sign of growing up is taking pride in what we do and how we do it.

~

How do I offer to help out at home?
How do I offer to help out at school?
Why is it important to be helpful and consistent?

~

Caring for Ourselves

Care is an important word. When we think about all the care that is provided for us as we grow up ... there is a lot involved like our food, clothing, shelter, love, rules, protection, education, boundaries, safety, and entertainment. At some point, when we're ready, we will learn to provide these things for ourselves. We will probably recall the way we were cared for ... so that we will know how to care for ourselves and others.

~

How am I independent in caring for myself today?
What have I learned from my past about caring for myself and others?

~

Staying "Young at Heart"

For kids ... life is about going from one fun event to the next. As we grow older and wiser ... our responsibilities begin to multiply. Chores and homework will eventually turn into jobs, careers, and college degrees. It's easy to begin to take ourselves so seriously that we forget how good it feels to laugh and be silly like when we were kids. Staying young at heart and remembering to have fun should come naturally. But some of us need permission. So here it is ... It's okay to laugh, be silly, and have fun ... while we're pursuing our goals and dreams. We must find our balance ... but stay on track!

~

Do I take myself too seriously?
What was the last thing I did that was fun and silly for no reason at all?

~

Being a Leader

It's hard to be told what to do all the time. It's probably easy to assume that being the boss will make us feel better. But being the boss isn't necessarily an easy job. It takes good leadership SKILLZ to be the boss. We must look at the entire picture and make decisions based on what's best for everyone ... not just ourselves. A good leader listens with patience, care, and understanding. And they're also willing to take responsibility for their mistakes ... without excuses. It takes a person of great character to make a great leader. So maybe being told what to do isn't so bad right now. Watch, listen, and learn.

~

Who's the best leader I know?
What makes this person a good leader?
Which of his or her leadership SKILLZ do I possess?

~

Trusting Our Parents

Some of us get angry when we get treated like children. Like when our parents stop talking when we walk into the room because they think we're too young to understand. Or when they make us turn the channel on the TV because the show we were watching is too "mature" for us. How about if they go through our things or try to listen in on our phone calls? That can be totally frustrating. However, we have to remember that our parents are doing the best they can. And they have our best interests in mind. So rather than act childish by rebelling against them … we should be wise and trust their judgment.

~

What do my parents do that makes me feel like a child?
Why do I think they do this?

~

Hormones!

Hormones are little chemical transmitters that change us emotionally and physically. When we are growing, our bodies get a blast of hormones that often send us into a tailspin of turmoil. It may seem like overnight we have been transformed into another person. For some of us, these changes can be a challenge to get used to … while others may rush into them. Just knowing that these changes take place in everyone and having acceptance and patience with ourselves as we start to change is a good sign that our reactions are maturing right along with the rest of us.

~

What changes am I going through right now?
What are my fears about these changes?
Whom can I talk to for support during this time?

~

Gaining Freedom

As we begin to do things on our own, we may start to feel as though we are ready to go it alone. But we shouldn't rush into adulthood … this is an opportunity to test our maturity. It is important that our parents allow us some freedoms to grow and change. However, they are watching us closely to see how we handle ourselves in different situations. The more freedom they give us, the more responsible we must be. Chances are, if we are consistently checking in with them and following through with our duties at home and school, they will continue to extend us more and more freedom. Gaining freedom is earned … by doing the right things.

~

Why do I think freedom should be earned instead of given?
What areas of my life would I like more freedom?
Why do I think I'm ready for more freedom?

~

CHAPTER 29: *Gratitude*

Easy Street

If we had everything — popularity, good looks, money, and great friends — we'd probably be spoiled, self-centered, and ungrateful. It's hard to be grateful when things come too easily. And it's hard to be humble if we have more than everyone around us. There is a certain sense of appreciation that comes from earning our rewards rather than having them given to us. If we were born on "easy street," we need to be grateful. If we weren't born on "easy street" … it's okay. Being thankful for what we have and when we achieve what we want for ourselves, gratitude will come naturally.

~

Why is it important to be grateful for what I have?
Why is it important to be humble?

~

For the Little Things

It's important to remember to have respect for the small things in our lives. Without a penny we could never have a dollar. Without the alphabet we wouldn't have books … and so on. The point is that everything has to start somewhere. So if we're thinking that what we have isn't enough … we shouldn't forget that when we minimize the importance of something, we rob ourselves of the potential of what it could become. We need to be grateful for the little things … they matter too.

~

What are the little things I am grateful for?
What little things do I take for granted?

~

Rules

Rules are everywhere. At home we have to keep our rooms clean and do our homework. Outside we have to cross at the crosswalk, obey traffic signals, and play fair. At school we have to be in class on time, dress in an appropriate manner, and respect the faculty and our peers. The truth is … all of the rules in our lives came from someone else's experience. Rules are enforced to help us avoid the painful price that someone else has already paid. Rules are like freebies. So, in a sense, we are benefiting from someone else's mistake. And for that we can be grateful.

~

What rules do I have a hard time with?
Why do I struggle in these areas?
What rules are easy for me to follow?

~

Thanks!

It's really awesome to have people in our lives that love us. Whether it's our family, friends or both, our support group is important because they are the ones who we look to for so many things. But because they're always there … it's easy to take them for granted … especially when things are good. That's why saying "thanks" to them should become a regular habit. Just hearing that word let's them know we're grateful. And saying it reminds us of how precious they are.

~

Whom do I rely on for support? Who relies on me for support?
Why is a support group important?

~

Make a Gratitude List

Making a gratitude list is one of the most powerful things we can do to change the way we view life. When things get tough, it's very easy to tell ourselves that everything's wrong and nothing ever goes our way. Even though this is far from true … sometimes it feels this way when we get disappointed. But if we write down all of the things we're grateful for, it's usually not long before our negative thoughts disappear and our minds open up to how good we really have it. So when we are feeling down, we need to make a gratitude list. This is something that we can use throughout our lives. It's simple, easy, quick, free, and it works.

~

Why do I think a gratitude list changes my thinking?
What happens if I am never grateful for what I have?

~

Tough Times

Some day, when we think about the tough times in our lives, we'll say … "I am so grateful that happened to me." Maybe not at this stage in our lives … but soon, we'll be able to look at the tough times in life and realize how they change us from the inside. How, as a person, we are different, because something happened to us. We'll be grateful because we're stronger as a result of going through it. This is a very "mature" concept. We may or may not be ready to understand this, but just know that gifts of life come in all different kinds of packages. So we must never discount the misfortunes in our lives; they may just be a gift we become grateful for later.

~

What's the toughest time I remember going through?
How did it change me? What did I learn from it?

~

Positive Attitude

If we have a negative attitude and we are looking for "what is wrong" in the world, we will probably find plenty. That can be depressing and sad or even make us angry. But if we try to keep a positive attitude, no matter what … we will find a lot of good in the world. It's not that bad things don't happen … they do. It's just that when we choose to focus on the good and be grateful … it makes the world a better place. It can make our world a better place.

~

What do I love about the world today?
What am I grateful for in my world today?
Why is it important to keep a positive attitude?

~

CHAPTER 30: *Happiness*

Laughter and Tears

A good hearty laugh is fun and contagious. Crying, however, isn't always so great. Whether emotionally or physically … believe it or not, crying is just as important as laughter for the human spirit. Even though it feels much more uncomfortable to cry, it allows us to express ourselves when something hurts, and can relieve the pressure that might otherwise come out in a misdirected way. Our emotions don't stay all bottled up inside. Laughter and tears are a part of our internal balance.

~

What was the last thing I had a good hearty laugh about?
What was the last thing I cried about?
Why is it healthy to laugh and cry?

~

Happiness and Joy

We might think happiness and joy are the same, but they are not. The deep down warmth we feel when we think about how much we love our family and friends is joy. Happiness comes from that feeling of excitement after hearing good news or doing something fun. Where happiness is only a temporary state of mind, joy can live in the heart forever.

~

What brings me joy? What makes me happy?

~

Smiling

When people smile at us for no reason ... it's nice to smile back. If we wonder what they're smiling about ... we may find the answer to be really simple. A warm thought, a funny memory, or an upcoming event could be the reason. Or maybe, someone smiled at them and they decided to pass it on. Just like laughter, smiling can be contagious. And much like good news, it can change our day. So ... don't forget to smile!

~

Why is smiling important?
What makes me smile most often?

~

An Inside Job

People often look outside of themselves for happiness. They assume that material things like money, beauty, and popularity will bring them self-worth. But the people who are truly secure with themselves will tell us that self-worth, lasting happiness, and freedom come from within. Anything outside of ourselves that can make us feel happy is usually temporary and can be taken away. So what happens when these things are gone? We're left with who we are and what we stand for. In other words ... it's an inside job. Material things will always be appealing ... but don't confuse them with the things that really matter.

~

What makes me feel secure?
What makes me feel insecure?

~

Life Isn't Perfect

Rarely will we ever find anything that is "perfect." And the harder we look for perfection, the more imperfection we will find. The pursuit of perfection can make life frustrating. On the other hand, happiness can be found easily when we are willing to accept that life isn't perfect and have gratitude for the little things that mean so much, like a hug, a smile, or an encouraging word. Expecting things to be perfect all the time just isn't realistic. Accepting things as they are brings happiness to a whole new level.

~

What does it mean to be "perfectly imperfect"?
Why is it unhealthy to pursue perfection?

~

Optimistic

There are two ways we can look at things: With a pessimistic attitude … meaning our glass is half empty, or with an optimistic attitude … meaning our glass is half full. Pessimists go through everyday routines with very little joy in their heart, nothing to look forward to, and a so-so attitude. Optimists, on the other hand, try their best, even when doing everyday things, finding joy and happiness all around and are a pleasure to spend time with. We have a choice. And good living starts when we choose an optimistic attitude.

~

Why is it important to have an optimistic attitude?
What does happiness have to do with being optimistic?
Do I need to change my attitude? Why or why not?

~

Sadness

Being a happy person doesn't mean that we don't feel sad sometimes. Everyone has sad times and challenges in life. It's normal to be unhappy and disappointed when things get tough. However, if we make a decision to remain stuck in negativity, then we are choosing sadness over happiness. And that's not necessary. There's no set time frame for feeling sad, but if we have chosen happiness as our foundation, then it shouldn't take too long before we want to move out of the darkness and back into the light. It may take a bit of practice. We must remember that what we focus on will dictate our mood. Once again … we have a choice.

~

Have I ever been "stuck" being sad?
What are some things I can do to change my mood?

~

Chapter 31: *Respect*

Privacy

It's important to respect people's right to privacy. While most of us would like to believe that we respect peoples' rights … there's a fine line between simple curiosity and a full-blown invasion. If we've ever listened in on other conversations without their permission … that's an invasion. If we've ever watched someone without his knowledge … that's also an invasion. And if we read something that wasn't meant for our eyes … well this is a clear example of an invasion of privacy. If we're not sure whether or not our behavior is acceptable, then we must ask ourselves … would it be okay if it were being done to us? And we'll get our answer.

~

Has someone ever read my diary, listened in on a phone call, or spied on me?
How did it feel?

~

Respect Ourselves

Treating ourselves with respect is one of the most powerful and loving things that we can do. If we make a mistake and call ourselves "stupid," that's not treating ourselves with respect. Any time that we put ourselves in an unsafe situation or allow anyone to treat us badly, we aren't respecting ourselves. And if we don't respect ourselves, others won't either. However, if we are patient, kind, and respectful to ourselves and others, it sets a standard for all to follow.

~

Do I know others who treats themselves with respect?
What do they do that I don't do?
What do I need to change to be more respectful to myself?

~

Family

The people in our lives that we spend the most time with are usually the ones we get the most upset with. When we feel comfortable around someone it's easier to allow our true feelings to show. And sometimes that can mean yelling at family members. Of course, we know they will love us anyway and forgive us when we ask, but that doesn't make it okay. Feeling angry is normal, but yelling is disrespectful. It's important to treat our families with the same respect we would give to someone else.

~

Who's the last family member I yelled at? Why did I yell?

~

Our Parents

When we have close friends, we get a chance to see how they interact with their parents. We might be shocked to learn that a friend of ours speaks disrespectfully to his or her parents. Being respectful to others is important. Being respectful to our parents is a must! We treat others with respect because it is how we want to be treated. If we find ourselves with the opportunity to give a friend some helpful advice, we should not be afraid to remind them that their parents are human and have feelings, too.

~

Why is it important to respect our parents?
How can I show respect to my parents?

~

Being Kind

Learning to choose our words carefully is an important aspect of being respectful. Words can hurt. Being kind to others is a sign of respect. Unfortunately, there are people who talk to others without any regard for their feelings. If we have something to say that may be uncomfortable for others ... we need to think about the best way to say it before we blurt it out. Take our time and try to stay away from blaming or accusing others. We can usually achieve a positive outcome if we say things in a positive way.

~

What are some examples of positive words?

~

The Golden Rule

Remember the golden rule ... treat others' as we want to be treated. Period. No exceptions. When we think about it ... it's a pretty tall order. But imagine what kind of place the world would be if everyone truly lived by this simple rule. Since no one wants to be treated badly, it's safe to say that if we all followed the golden rule, we could do away with hatred, war, crime, and so on. The possibilities are endless. And it all starts with us.

~

What can I do to make a difference?
How do I live by the golden rule today?
Who are the people in my life who live by the golden rule?

~

Authority

Some people just refuse to respect authority, but here is the reality … whether or not we like the rules doesn't really matter. The only thing that does matter is whether or not we respect authority and play by the rules.. Some people may think that freedom means they should be able to do what they want, when they want. But we live in a society where if people simply did what they wanted to do — without consequences — it would be a disaster! Laws, rules, guidelines, and boundaries are necessary to create order. And people in authority enforce those rules for our protection. So unless our plan is to move into the jungle and live like animals where there are no rules … we might as well respect the authority in our community and save ourselves some trouble.

~

Who are the authority figures in my community?
What are the rules I find difficult to follow?
What are the rules I find easy to follow?
Do I struggle with authority? Why or why not?

~

CHAPTER 32: *Relationships*

Arguments

Most of us feel uncomfortable when people start to argue. That's normal. Arguments are hard to watch especially when it's someone that we love. Disagreements are a part of life. And so is making up. Sometimes arguments are necessary to clear the air. Sometimes it can pave the way for a better relationship. When we learn to accept this. It won't bother us so much.

~

Have people ever argued in front of me?
How did it make me feel?
Who was the last person I argued with?
How did I resolve the argument?

~

Confrontations

Confrontations are very difficult. If someone causes us harm, or oversteps a boundary, it needs to be confronted. Whenever we have to talk to people about something they said or did … it may feel uncomfortable. We may tell ourselves that it's easier not to say anything … and it is. But it's not healthy and it's not fair to us or others. When we tell someone the truth about how we feel, even when we're afraid, we are taking care of ourselves. And we're giving the relationship a chance to grow. Confrontations don't have to end in disaster. It's actually how we show others that we care enough to be honest.

~

When was my last confrontation? What was it about?
How did I take care of myself in this situation?

~

Infatuation

Sometimes we meet people we really, really like and find ourselves thinking about them all the time. It's common to meet others who totally grab our attention. Maybe they are so different from us that we find them fascinating. Or maybe it's just their personalities or even their looks that attract us. Whatever it is, remember that everyone needs their space. No matter how infatuated we are … we had a life before we met them. If they are meant to be a part of our lives, they will be. We mustn't forget about our friends, families, and commitments.

~

Who was the first person I was infatuated with?
What about that person impressed me?
How do I feel about that person now?

~

Friends

Friendship is the most special kind of relationship. Some flow very easily, while others can require work to maintain. But no friendship should be a constant struggle. If we find that we just aren't getting along with someone anymore … it's okay to take a step back and give the relationship some space. We should never try to force people to be who we want them to be. Nor should we ever try to change for someone else. The best relationships go through their ups and downs. We must be true to ourselves and allow things to take their natural course.

~

What kind of friend am I?
Am I true to myself in my relationships?
Do I allow others to be themselves?

~

When it's Time to Move On

Sometimes relationships go from good to bad. Whether we are ready to move on or the other person is, we have to know when to let go. There isn't always a grand explanation. All relationships begin and end. It's what we have in between that really matters. The way we show up in a relationship and what we learn from it is so much more fulfilling when we can accept that it has come to an end and let it go with love. If we or the other person is holding on in a desperate attempt to control the outcome, we both will be left with bitter memories. It doesn't mean we won't feel sad when it ends. But there's a difference between allowing ourselves to feel sad, and creating drama because we can't accept reality. When it becomes overly complicated … it's time to move on.

~

How do I describe my best relationship?
How do I describe my worst relationship?

~

A Struggle

Some people find themselves in a constant struggle to maintain their relationships. If we're wondering whether or not we're one of these people, it might be time to take a look at how we interact with others. Do we always have to have things go our way? Do we need to be right in every discussion? Does it seem our friendships don't last very long? The common thread is … US. No one enjoys being in a relationship with someone who drains them or treats them unfairly. So if we find that we're on the giving or receiving end of this kind of struggle, it's time to make a change.

~

How would I describe most of my relationships?
Do I struggle to maintain any of my friendships?
Am I clingy or controlling?
Do my friendships last?

~

Meaningful Relationships

Being honest, trustworthy, humble, caring, and giving are the qualities that make for great relationships. There are many more as well, but these key ingredients will make our relationships meaningful and long lasting. When both people are contributing their best qualities to a relationship, it becomes a very special gift. Once we experience this kind of relationship, we'll be more attracted to people who possess good qualities and less attracted to ones who don't.

~

What's missing in my relationships?
What do I need to change to make my relationships more meaningful?

~

Chapter 33: *Quiet Time*

It's Important

Some people lead such busy lives that there's very little time to take a look at themselves. When we reflect on where we stand with our day, our week, our problems, and our blessings, we'll need some quiet time. Quiet time will help give us clarity on our strengths, our weaknesses, and what we'd like to change. We need to take the time to examine our lives and how we spend our time. Get our priorities straight. Clear our heads. Watch ourselves grow.

~

What are the good aspects of my life?
What would I like to change? How can I change it?

~

Downtime

Everyone needs and deserves a little downtime. The more we live our lives on the go … the more downtime we should have. Some of us are afraid that we'll miss something if we don't show up for everything. But the truth is that even though it's important to live a full and abundant life, we need rest and relaxation to be able to truly appreciate what we have. Otherwise we'll burn out and spend all our energy just "going through the motions." Stay in our PJs one day and do nothing. Spend a weekend with no plans. Give our bodies and our brains some well-deserved rest. Schedule some downtime.

~

Am I afraid of missing something?
When do I find myself "running on empty"? Why is downtime important?

~

Meditating

Meditation is a form of quiet time that helps us get in touch with our true hearts' desires. In our busy lives, we need down time and quiet time to keep a positive attitude and a clear perspective. In our busy minds, we use meditation to clear away negative thoughts so we can focus on the important things, the things that are important in our hearts. For those of us who aren't quite sure what our true hearts desires are, meditation is the perfect way to get in touch with this. It may be a little uncomfortable at first ... but just like anything, the more we do it the easier it becomes. Start with a quiet place, turn everything off and just breathe deeply. Give it five minutes and after a few times, try to increase it to ten. It might seem pointless at first but if we stick with it, we will definitely receive the countless benefits of meditation.

~

What do I think I might get out of meditating?
Why is meditation important?
Am I willing to give meditation a try? Why or why not?

~

Alone Time

Some of us don't like to be alone. We may find it boring. Sometimes it's easier to be surrounded by people, because then we don't have to focus on ourselves. But alone time can be very valuable. When we're alone we can read, write, rest, think, or daydream. We can learn to be a friend to ourselves and practice enhancing our lives instead of being distracted by the lives of those around us. When we can learn to enjoy our own company, we will become more confident and self-reliant. And when we get out into the world, we will attract people who are the same.

~

Am I afraid to be alone? Why or why not?
What does it mean to "become your own best friend"?

~

The Great Outdoors

Fresh air, sunlight, and blue skies are just a small part of the beauty that nature has to offer. Experiencing the great outdoors is a great way to slow down for a minute and remove ourselves from the stress of our everyday lives. There's nothing that can so easily change our perspective as heading outdoors. Taking a quick walk, eating our lunch in the grass, listening to the sounds of nature, or just surrounding ourselves with the warming effect of the sun can quickly put us in a peaceful state of mind. Plan some quiet time outside and allow Mother Nature to refuel our spirit. We will probably be able to complete the rest of our day with a new attitude.

~

What do I like best about being outdoors?
Why do I think nature has a claiming effect on us?

~

Restful Sleep

We may not realize how important a good night's sleep is. Not everyone gets enough sleep and a lot of people don't sleep well when they do sleep. Nightmares, unhealthy eating habits, and stress are just a few of the things that can keep us from a restful sleep. Sleeping is probably the most important quiet time that we'll ever get. Without restful sleep, most people are irritable, angry, overly emotional and just harder to be around. Sleep rejuvenates the mind, body, and spirit. We can't last long without it. Make sure we get at least eight hours of sleep and take the time to consider any habits of ours that might be affecting the quality of our sleep.

~

Do I get at least eight hours of sleep every night?
Do I have any bad eating habits that may affect my sleep?

~

Silence is Golden

When we think about all of the noise in the world ... it's amazing that anyone can think at all. From television, telephones, radios, and talking ... there's enough noise to keep us far away from any form of quiet time. When we turn off all the electronics and we're totally alone, we may feel the need to create some noise. But it's extremely healthy to listen to the silence. The sound of our breathing, the beat of our hearts, and a quiet mind will help us stay centered. We live in a noisy society. It's normal to walk in the house and turn something on. But see what happens when we don't turn anything on. Stay in the silence and learn to embrace everything about ourselves.

~

Does silence bother me? What do I think about when I'm alone?
Am I comfortable by myself? Why or why not?

~

CHAPTER 34: *Forgiveness*

It's about US

When others cause us harm, it's not always easy to forgive. Forgiving others who harmed us will probably help them feel better, but the real bonus to forgiveness is that we will feel better, too. It takes a lot of energy to stay mad at someone. We may spend time thinking about it, avoiding that person and even talking about him behind his back. But once we extend forgiveness … our hearts will be lighter and the drama will be over. Forgiveness is as much about us as it is about the person being forgiven.

~

Is there someone who needs my forgiveness?
Is there someone I'd like to forgive me?
Why is forgiveness so powerful?

~

Hurt Feelings

Some people are very sensitive and get their feelings hurt easily. Even if we're not one of the sensitive types … hurt feelings are a part of life. Sometimes it may seem like people hurt us on purpose. But when we think hard about it, we will realize we've probably hurt someone's feelings before without meaning to. With that in mind, a little forgiveness goes a long, long way.

~

What was the last situation that hurt my feelings?
How did I resolve the situation?

~

Compassion

When others hurt us or make us angry, we might tell ourselves that we will NEVER forgive them. We may decide to cut them out of our lives forever. But is that how we really feel? Most likely … it's not. Once we've let some time pass, we may find that we don't feel as angry anymore. We may even try to understand why the others did what they did. This is when we are practicing compassion rather than judgment. When we can put our own feelings aside long enough to see someone else's view, we might be surprised to discover how quickly forgiveness takes over.

~

What is the difference between compassion and judgment?
Why is judgment so harmful?
Why do compassion and forgiveness go hand in hand?

~

Patience

When we're the one who caused harm, we usually think we should be forgiven right away. We may even become intolerant of the idea that we have to wait for forgiveness. But it helps to remember that just like us, people might need time because the healing process takes time … (for both parties). So we must be patient with them.

~

Why do I think it takes time to heal?
Has anyone ever decided not to forgive me for something?

~

Free Ourselves

Forgiveness is not about letting others off the hook for what they did. It's about us not holding on to what they did anymore. It's easy to justify holding on to anger ... especially if we're trying to teach the others a lesson. But the longer we carry around anger inside, the harder it will be for us to be happy. Anger holds the happiness hostage ... while forgiveness holds the key to our freedom. It's okay to let it go and move on.

~

Am I ever an angry person? When?
How can I let go of my anger?

~

Without Judgment

When we forgive others for something, a simple ... "I accept your apology" will do. If we need to remind others of how horrible they were first, then we're missing the point. Forgiveness is about compassion and humility. Not judgment and arrogance. When others ask for forgiveness, they are acknowledging their wrongs and are trying to mend the situation. If we're not ready to accept the apology, well, that's okay. Let people learn their own lessons without judging them ... just as we have.

~

Why is judgment such a negative thing?
Who have I judged recently? Why did I do this?

~

Forgiving Ourselves

How do we treat ourselves when we make a mistake? Sometimes the hardest person to forgive is ourselves. It's important to take a look at what we'd like to change and make the corrections where needed. That's part of taking ownership. But we don't want to be so hard on ourselves that we feel shame and guilt each time we make a mistake. When we make a mistake, acknowledge it, make the changes, forgive ourselves … then let it go and learn from it.

~

What mistake have I made over and over again?
What mistake have I learned from and what did I learn?
How do I forgive myself when I make a mistake?

~

CHAPTER 35: *Discipline*

The Road to Success

We all have a secret something that we wished we were good at. Unfortunately, the road to success is not paved with wishing. Any successful person will tell us that discipline and hard work are the key ingredients to being really good at something. If we commit to practicing fifteen minutes a day for thirty days, we may be amazed at what we can do.

~

What am I really good at?
What would I like to be really good at?
What does discipline mean to me?

~

Make a Change

If we find ourselves getting punished over and over for the same thing, then it's time to make a change. If we keep doing what we've always done, then we'll continue to pay the same price. Doing something different requires discipline. Most of us already know what is the right thing to do. However, giving in to temptations can be a hard habit to break. So the next time we're about to indulge in the very thing that continues to get us into trouble ... we should stop and ask ourselves ... "What happened the last time I did this?" Hopefully, our experience — along with some discipline — will save us from future pain.

~

What bad habits are hard for me to break?
Why does making a change require discipline?

~

Focus

When we are in the middle of doing something and we get tired or bored, focusing will give us the strength and energy to finish what we started. Focus! We can go further if we let our minds take over. When we focus on the task at hand, and tell ourselves to stick with it, our bodies will respond. This is called discipline. And with a little discipline the possibilities are endless.

~

What do I find hard to focus on?
What do I need to focus on more?

~

Temperance

Now here's a word we won't hear every day. Temperance is about having balance and doing things in moderation. When we know that too much of any one thing is not good for us, it takes discipline to practice temperance. Restrain ourselves a little, create a balance in our lives and we'll be able to enjoy and appreciate things so much more.

~

What do I do too much of?
What area could use more of my attention?
Whom do I know has temperance in her or his life?

~

Knowing Who We Are ...

Having some discipline in our lives is a lot easier if we know who we are and when we're at our best. If we are a morning person but we've committed to doing certain tasks in the evening, we may get stressed out and disappointed when we can't follow through with things. Maybe we should try doing them in the morning instead. Knowing when we are most productive can help us accomplish things easier. Getting to know ourselves better will help make the most of our efforts.

~

What three words describe the best parts of my personality?
What three words describe the worst parts of my personality?
What three words would I like to be able to use when describing myself?

~

Who Will We Be?

It's up to us to decide what kind of person we want to be. The decisions we make now will help determine who we will be tomorrow. We may be the only one standing in the way of our dreams. There will always be obstacles along the way; however, the way we choose to handle them can mean the difference between using the lesson to our advantage ... or allowing it to stop us. It's up to us to use some discipline and stay focused, no matter what. Find something that moves us, something we're passionate about and go for it.

~

What kind of person do I want to be?
Why does it require discipline to follow our dreams?

~

Be Gentle with Ourselves

It's possible to push ourselves too hard. We must remember that no one is perfect. As we start practicing discipline in our lives, we want to remember that being too critical with ourselves is as destructive as not trying at all. Although discipline is one of the greatest tools for success, we can overdo it. We should remember to be kind and gentle to ourselves along the way.

~

What does it mean to be too critical of ourselves?
What does it mean to be gentle with ourselves?

~

CHAPTER 36: *Fitting In*

Finding Our Place

Most people hang out with people based on the music they like, the sports they play, or the other things they have in common. Sometimes we're not sure where we fit in. Some of us try really hard to fit into places where it just doesn't work. This can be painful. It hurts because we don't want to be left out. But there is a place where we fit in perfectly ... we just need to keep looking. Try new things, talk to new people, and before we know it, we've found our place in society.

~

Who are the people I fit in with?
What do I have in common with them?
What other things am I interested in?

~

People Pleasing

Everyone wants to be liked by others. But some people go to extreme lengths just to be liked. They might pretend to have the same opinions as others ... or even try to buy people's friendship with money or compliments. "People pleasing" is a very subtle form of dishonesty. It's dishonest, because we're not being the real us and other people like someone they don't really know. We should not underestimate our value. We can be ourselves around people and let our true spirit shine. True connections don't have to be controlled ... they happen naturally.

~

Who have I 'people-pleased' in the past?
Why did I try to control their impression of me?
What will I do differently in the future?

~

When it's Time to Tell

Some of us were "tattletales" growing up. It sounds pretty silly now, because with maturity we've learned where to draw the line between what's our responsibility and what's none of our business. Telling people's business is just another desperate attempt to fit in. However, if someone is hurting us or anyone else … we need to tell. That's the bottom line. Hurting someone or planning to hurt someone is unacceptable. Knowing when to tell could potentially save someone from harm.

~

What have I told someone that was none of my business?
What should I have done instead?
Are there any secrets I'm keeping that could cause harm?

~

Gossip

Talking about people to fit in is a bad idea. Gossip can hurt people. If we catch ourselves talking about someone and following it with a "please don't say anything," then we're obviously gossiping. The golden rule here is … if we wouldn't say it to his or her face, then we shouldn't be saying it at all. Being the first one with juicy information about someone might make us look important for the moment … but people never forget who they can and cannot trust.

~

Who have I gossiped about in the past?
How did I feel when I was the topic of gossip?

~

Friendship

Friendship is one of the most valuable treasures in life. Having someone to laugh with, cry with, share with, and be there for is essential to fitting in and feeling a part of something special. True friendship is a two-way street. If we're doing all of the taking or all of the giving, then we're not in a real friendship. We're in a relationship that we will soon resent. Make sure that our friends bring out the best in us and we do the same for them. If we want to have good friends, we have to be a good friend.

~

What kind of friend am I?
What's my idea of a good friendship?
Who are my closest friends?

~

Helping the Underdog

We probably all know someone at school, or in our neighborhoods who just doesn't fit in. Maybe they're always alone or just a little on the dorky side. Some of us may have even been that kid. And some of us may have avoided being seen with that kid. But chances are … we all have felt like that kid at one time or another. What if we were friends with that kid? Or defended that kid when others weren't being nice to him? We would be showing compassion, rather than judgment. We would be supportive, rather than making his life harder. Everyone needs and deserves to fit in. So what kind of people are we? Do we have enough courage to help the underdog?

~

Who is the underdog in my school/neighborhood?
What can I do to help them fit in?

~

Go with the Flow

Hanging out with our friends can be one of the best parts of our youth. When everyone decides to get together, a key part to fitting in is to go with the flow. If two friends want to go to the movies and we'd rather go to the mall … it's okay to simply surrender and go to the movies. If we find ourselves constantly pushing for everyone to do what we want to do, or pouting when we get out-voted, then we might find that we'll stop getting invited to hang out with everyone. Being controlling and disruptive will never be popular. So unless our friends are doing something that goes against our morals … learn to go with the flow rather than against it.

~

When is it easy for me to go with the flow?
When is it hard for me to go with the flow?
What's the difference between going with the flow and people-pleasing?

~

CHAPTER 37: *Family*

Accepting Them

Are we embarrassed by our family's behavior? Like when our mom tries to act cool and be one of the girls? Or when our brother or sister starts showing off when our friends come over? These are the times when we desperately do not want to be associated with our families. Or at the very least, we would like to be able to control their behavior. But the truth is, we can't control anyone but ourselves. So what can we do? Well, we can practice not reacting to them. We can learn to love and accept them the way they are, even when they embarrass us. If we want people to accept us the way we are ... then we need to learn to do the same for them.

~

How does my family cause me embarrassment?
Do I cause my family embarrassment? How?

~

Family Time

Spending a certain time with our family each week is very important, whether it is a whole day or just a certain meal that we always get to spend together. This time can be special because it is how we connect with each other regularly. We can talk about our week and maybe share some good times or get advice about anything we might be having trouble with. These family gatherings will create cherished memories that will last the rest of our lives. We can't take time with our loved ones for granted!

~

What do I love to do with my family?
What would I like to do more of with my family?

~

Learn to Laugh

Although we all would like to go through life without an embarrassing moment … it's probably not going to happen. So the best thing we can do is not take ourselves too seriously and learn to laugh at ourselves. A safe place to start practicing this is with our families. Whether we fall down in front of them, get caught with lettuce in our teeth, listen to them tell the same humiliating story about us over and over again, burp, or worse … most of us have had to endure some teasing from a loved one. So rather than get angry and plot some kind of revenge, we can stop taking ourselves so seriously and join in the fun. Laugh with them.

~

What's the most embarrassing story my family tells about me?
Why do I find this story so humiliating?

~

My Family Seems So Different from Other Families

The most unique thing about our families is … that it's our family. Some of us watch other people interact with their families and wonder why our family seems so different. The truth is, someone may have watched us with our family and thought the same thing. Every family has its strengths and weaknesses. And every family has a "crazy Aunt" they don't want anyone to meet. If we have to judge our family, let's base it on how they support and love us. We can't make comparisons with other families. Look at the things that make our family unique and be grateful.

~

What are my family's strengths? What are my family's weaknesses?
What makes my family unique?

~

Unconditional Love

Going through a rough time is when we need unconditional love the most. None of us feel good about ourselves when we're paying the price for bad behavior. But the unconditional love of our family can get us through it. No matter what the situation is, or how destructive our actions were, we should be able to be honest with our family without fear of judgment. Let them know that we need their unconditional love. Then love ourselves without conditions. This might require a little practice before it is comfortable, but when we show unconditional love to ourselves and others, it becomes contagious!

~

What does unconditional love mean to me?
When was the last time that I needed unconditional love?
When was the last time I gave unconditional love?

~

Being Supportive

It's very easy to point out what someone else is doing wrong, especially with family ... because we spend so much time with them. Some of us might tend to jump in and try to fix the problem since we have such a clear view of what needs to change. Even with the best intentions, trying to point out or fix a problem for a family member may not be the healthiest approach to helping them. Most times simply being supportive is enough. This might entail just listening with an open mind or giving them a reassuring hug. Everyone has their own struggles therefore everyone learns their own lessons. Learn what it means so be supportive and start practicing now.

~

How have I tried to "fix" peoples' problems?
Who in my family tries to fix my problems?
What can I change so that I am simply being supportive?

~

The In-between Years

When we are a tween or a teen, we may feel stuck in the middle. We know that we are no longer kids, yet we are not quite adults, either. Being in between poses a separate set of problems. This is most likely the only time we will ever feel this way. This is a preparation period. We are very close to being on our own. We're beginning to make decisions for ourselves and act independently. However, our parents know that there is still much for us to learn. Don't forget that they've walked this path before us and they're on our side. Some of the things that they've been telling us repeatedly won't actually make sense until later. But someday… it will make sense. This is our opportunity to test our SKILLZ, not run the show. So we must be patient with our families and take our time with decisions. Let them love us through the in-between years.

~

Am I rushing to grow-up and be on my own? Why or why not?
What decisions am I afraid to make for myself?
What decisions am I anxious to make for myself?

~

CHAPTER 38: *Friends*

Give and Take

When a friendship is unbalanced … it will eventually be a burden to both parties. Both people have to give a little and take a little for the friendship to work. If we're doing all the talking, making all the decisions and not allowing our friend any input, then our friendship is out of balance. And it's equally as unhealthy for the friend who's doing all the listening and allowing themselves to be a doormat. No matter which one we are, if this describes one or more of our friendships, then it's time to make some changes before the resentments start. Give and take is what makes most relationships work.

~

How would I describe my friendships?
Why is it important that both people give a little and take a little?

~

Be a Part of the Solution

When we find out that people have been "bashing" us behind our backs, it can be very painful. We may tell ourselves that these people weren't real friends. On the other hand … most of us have at the very least, participated in gossip or bashed one of our friends on occasion. Even if we were only doing it to fit in … it's wrong. When we're bashing someone … or we're the one being bashed … there's a problem. However, we can be a part of the solution by walking away or speaking up and saying "Hey! Let's talk about something else!" And should we hear about something that was said behind our backs, we can go directly to that person and ask them not to do again. That's being a part of the solution. It may not be the 'popular' thing to do, but it's definitely the right thing.

~

Who have I 'bashed' or gossiped about? Why?

~

What Happened?

A friend stops calling and we start to wonder … did we do something? So we call to find out what happened and our friend says … "nothing happened." But still there's a distance between us. Once we've determined that we have been a good friend and have done nothing wrong, it might be time for a little acceptance. Sometimes people find new interests and sometimes people simply outgrow each other. But even if it doesn't have anything to do with us, it's hard not to take these things personally … and it might hurt for a while. But these changes are a part of life. And it won't hurt forever. So when someone decides to move on, there's not much we can do about it except move on, too.

~

Have I outgrown a friend in my past?
Is there a friend I was very close to but I'm not anymore?
What changed in these friendships?

~

Life Lessons

We've probably all had friends move away whom we don't see much anymore. It can feel very lonely when a friend leaves our lives. Often a new friendship develops as we let go of the old one. Or we might seek out new friends so the void isn't so great. These are the lessons that prepare us for adulthood. As we go through life, we will have many friends who come and go. Some we may manage to keep a long distance communication with … and some we will only have fond memories of. But all of our friends … past, present, and future, will enhance our lives and help us grow somehow.

~

Which friends have helped me grow as a person? How?
What's the most valuable lesson I've learned from a friend?

~

Diversity

Diversity among friends is an asset. Each of us has our own unique and special gift to offer. And hopefully our group of friends possess a wide range of personalities and talents. Some friends are great listeners and good at calming us down, while others will keep us laughing. Some are wise and full of great advice while others will cheer us on no matter what. We need to figure out what our friends are good at and then network with them so that everyone is receiving the benefit of diversity.

~

What is my special gift to my friends?
Why is diversity among friends important?

~

Best Friends

Our "best" friend is the person who knows us better than anyone, the one who thinks like us and has a lot in common with us. Our best friend is probably the relationship that is the most fulfilling out of all our friendships. But it is also the one that can hurt us the most. As we grow up and learn to be vulnerable with people, our level of commitment to relationships will deepen. For most of us, this starts with a best friend. Once our heart commits to the friendship it's not so easy to walk away and it shouldn't be. If trouble arises … we should be willing to work through it if we're calling this person our best friend. This special friendship will help us learn to cope with relationships in a mature, responsible way.

~

Who is my best friend? Why is he (she) my best friend?
What have I learned from this friendship?

~

Having Fun

Having fun with our friends can be an awesome release from our daily routine. Good times are an essential part of friendship. However, it's easy to get carried away and forget that there's more to a friendship than having fun. Friends should enhance each other by being responsible and supportive. We can study with our friends, get to know each other's families and offer help when it's needed. A good friend will also care about what kind of grades we're getting and will encourage us to make healthy choices. Too much fun can easily turn into trouble. So if we find ourselves … or one of our friends … in a situation that's getting out of hand, we must be a responsible friend and listen to that inner voice telling us when enough is enough.

~

What do my friends and I do for fun?
How do I encourage my friends?
Who's the most responsible one in my group of friends? Why?

~

CHAPTER 39: *Goals*

Make a Plan

It is never too soon to think about a career. Some people know what they want to be when they grow up from the time they're in kindergarten. Other people stumble upon something they're passionate about and some people need suggestions thrown their way. Whatever we decide on, we will need a plan of how we want to achieve our goals. This may include getting good grades in high school so we can get a scholarship and be accepted into the college of our choice. Or some volunteer work to help shape our character. It may also include a summer job to gain some real-life experiences. Whatever our goals are for a career, we must start with a plan. What we decide to do today will directly affect our futures.

~

What are my plans for the future?
How will this help me in my career choice?

~

Positive Characteristics

There is more to goals than choosing a career. We also get to choose what kind of people we want to be and what kind of people we'd like to attract. Honesty, kindness, responsibility, and humility are just a few of the characteristics that we're learning to use in our everyday lives. Our goals to become and remain good people are just as important as our career goals. Once we realize the value of positive characteristics ... we'll be able to use them in every area of our lives.

~

What are my positive characteristics? What are my negative characteristics?
What am I doing to change the negative ones?

~

Changing Our Mind is Okay

It's hard not to be disappointed if we've found that we weren't very good at something we thought we would be. But there's no need to worry. Life is full of opportunities and experiences. If we set a goal for ourselves that just isn't working … it's okay to change our minds. That's the great thing about taking responsibility for our own decisions. Nothing is ever written in stone. Many professional writers started out as actors and many successful small business owners started out in medical school. The best way to find out if we will like what we've chosen … is to spend some time volunteering in the field in which we're interested. Once we know whether or not it's the right career for us … we'll know what the next step is.

~

What are three careers I am most drawn toward?
Why am I drawn to these particular careers?
How can I get some experience in these careers?

~

Goal-oriented

If we are goal-oriented, then we probably always have our eye on the prize. Whether that means getting the best grade, winning a game, or finishing a race, people who have goals can usually get a lot accomplished because they finish what they start. But when we are only focused on the prize, we may miss the joy of the journey. It's important to remember, as we stay focused on our goals, that we make one of our goals … to enjoy ourselves along the way.

~

Who do I know that is "goal-oriented"? What can I learn from them?
Why is it important to enjoy myself while pursuing my goals?

~

Baby Steps

The easiest way to tackle a big goal is to break it down into baby steps. Some of us get overwhelmed when we discover how much work is needed to achieve a goal. However, when we break the plan down into "baby steps," it becomes obtainable. We can apply that same logic to almost anything we want to do in life. Having a realistic goal is important for success. If we try to tackle too much at once we may fall. When we take things one step at a time ... it helps us stay on track.

~

What does it mean to break goals down into baby steps?
What other areas of my life sometimes overwhelms me?

~

No Regrets

Even if we don't meet our goals, or must change them, we should never have regrets. It's common to feel that we should be farther along than we are. However, it's not healthy, especially if we've been comparing ourselves to other people. It's never too late to try a different approach. And we can't put a price on experience; we just need to get back up if we fall or we are not successful the first time. Nothing is ever a waste of time as long as we continue to move in a positive direction.

~

Are there things in life that I regret? Why do I regret these things?
What lessons did I learn from these experiences?

~

Keep it Real

Just about everyone dreams of being rich and famous. If we dream of being a dancer …
we must dance! No one will ever be able to take away our passion for something. There's
absolutely nothing wrong with setting goals to try and achieve some form of super stardom,
but it's also important to keep it real. We can't all be rock stars, professional athletes, or super
models. For most of us, this means having some type of a back-up plan, because no matter
how talented we are … the odds of being rich and famous are not in our favor. So keep it
real. We must be sure to invest some time into other ways that we can earn a good living for
ourselves … just in case this super stardom thing doesn't work out.

~

If I could be a "superstar" what would I be?
What other areas in this same field interest me?

~

CHAPTER 40: *Bullies*

Who Are They?

Recognizing a bully isn't as easy as we might think it is. We might picture a bully as a big mean kid who picks on the small fragile kids. And although that description would fit some bullies, it can be much more than that. Bullies can be very subtle and manipulative. It might be the prettiest girl in our class or the kid with the biggest house. Whenever someone is continuously and purposely messing with us just to be mean … that is abusive. And that is a bully. It is wrong and it needs to stop.

~

What do I picture a bully looking like?
Do I know any bullies at my school?
Has anyone ever bullied me?

~

What Are They Thinking?

Bullies want and need to feel important because they tend to have very low self-esteem. Picking on others is a way for them to have power and exert control in their own lives. If they can make us look and feel bad … then they somehow feel important. It is quite twisted but easy to understand. People who are feared … feel important in a sick kind of way. They have a need for control. They need help.

~

How could I help a bully?
How could I help someone who is being bullied?

~

Am I a Bully?

If our behavior is mean, rude, or violent … if our behavior includes teasing others with the purpose of making them feel bad about themselves, especially in front of others … then it's very possible that we are bullies. Even if this behavior started out as innocent fun, bullying is abusive and can create major destruction for everyone. It's important to be aware of why we're doing it and the so-called power trip that it takes us on. It's easy to get carried away at someone else's expense, but hurting others is the wrong way to feel better about ourselves. So if we find that we're the one doing the bullying … it's important for us to stop.

~

Have I ever gotten carried away with teasing someone?
How do I know if I'm a bully?

~

How to Stop a Bully

Bullying is now so commonplace that it is being talked about in every school. It's no longer a dark secret. If we are being bullied, we need to tell an adult. It is our responsibility to tell. And if that adult doesn't do anything … we need to tell another adult. We must continue to talk about it until someone offers a solution. There is help available, but we have to ask. This is very important. Secrets tend to grow in the dark … but they die in the light. No matter how overwhelming it may seem, or how embarrassed we may feel … we need to be strong. At least strong enough to ask for help.

~

Why am I embarrassed or scared to tell on a bully?
Who can I talk to if I need to tell on a bully?

~

Know Who We Are

We all have strengths and weaknesses. Bullies will zero in on one particular weakness and then badger away. If we are being bullied … we cannot let what is happening define who we are. Just because someone may have decided to point out a weakness of ours does not mean that they are correct. Bullies operate through manipulation. We cannot allow ourselves to believe what a bully may be saying to us or about us. We are solely responsible for bringing ourselves back to the truth. We must remind ourselves of our good qualities. Focus on the people in our lives who love and respect us. Something may be happening to us but it is not who we are. And that is what is important. This will not always be a part of our lives. If we refuse to give it power, we will be so much stronger when it's over.

~

How can I become stronger after being bullied?
What can I learn from being bullied?
Why is it important to focus on the positive things?

~

Cyber-bullying

What makes cyber-bullying so dangerous? It is much easier for bullies to say mean things to us when they are not looking at us. Bullies are cowards. And cyber-space is the easiest place for a coward. Bullies on social networks have the ability to humiliate others and destroy their lives with the push of a few keys. It's a very serious problem. If we are on either end of this type of activity it needs to stop right now.

~

Have I ever participated in cyber-bullying?
Why is it so harmful to tell someone's personal business to everyone?
What's the difference between gossiping and cyber-bullying?

~

A Matter of Life and Death

When teasing and taunting goes too far … innocent people can be hurt and even destroyed. Whether we are a bully or we are being bullied … this epidemic has become a matter of life and death. Every year teens are killed while being bullied and from the effects of being bullied. Some even become so desperate that they see no way out except to take their own lives. What's so deeply frightening about this is that most people won't know the amount of harm caused … until it's too late. Any form of bullying is dangerous.

~

Have I ever heard of someone losing his or her life because of bullying?
How do I feel about bullying?
How can I protect myself from bullying?
Why is focusing on bullying a waste of time?

~

CHAPTER 41: *Self-Esteem*

Purpose

Having high self-esteem means we believe that we matter in this world. If we don't believe this about ourselves, then it's time to make a change. It helps if we believe we were made on purpose for a purpose. Finding our purpose in life doesn't have to be a struggle and our purpose may change and grow as we do. Every time we touch someone's life with love, laughter, or kindness, we've made a difference in both of our lives. And making a difference helps build self-esteem.

~

Do I believe I have a purpose?
How do I make a difference at home? At school? In my community?

~

Money!

Some people use money to build self-esteem. They think the more money they have the more cool stuff they'll have, the cooler they look, and the better they'll feel. This thinking is a lie. While having money gives us the freedom to buy what we want, being able to buy what we want does not make us better people. Treating people with respect, making healthy choices, following through with commitments, and helping others is how to become a better person and build self-esteem. Don't confuse looking good with feeling good. If we truly want to feel good about ourselves ... money has nothing to do with it.

~

Do I believe that having money makes me happy? Why or why not?

~

Validation

Some people fall into the bad habit of expecting others to give them validation; that is, making them feel important. When our self-esteem comes only from what other people say ... then we're in real trouble. This can be the beginning of a vicious cycle. It's always nice to hear people say good things about us. But unless we learn to say these things to ourselves, the happiness will only last a short time. Eventually we will find ourselves desperate to be validated by someone. When we think enough of ourselves to be honest, follow our dreams, and love ourselves just the way we are, we won't need anyone else's validation. Because we will be able to validate ourselves and that's the way it should be.

~

How do I validate myself?
Why is it important not to depend on other people for validation?

~

Pushing Ourselves

People are capable of doing much more than they realize. And goals that give us the biggest payoff usually require the most effort. Choosing goals that require real effort will probably make us feel the best about ourselves. This is because when we have the courage to dream big ... we have to push ourselves just a little harder. We may have to give up a night of hanging out ... or turn off the TV in order to focus on what we want to achieve, but if we're willing to challenge ourselves and push ourselves, we may be amazed at what we can accomplish and the self-esteem we will build. Remember that we will only get out of something ... what we're willing to put into it.

~

What are my dreams for the future? What am I doing to achieve my goals?
What can I do to push myself a little harder?

~

Friends

There's no such thing as self-esteem by association. If we find ourselves hanging out with a certain crowd because they look or act cool, or have cool stuff, then we are using them to build our own self-esteem. It will never work. Our friendships should be based on common interests and mutual respect. Our self-esteem will grow when we learn to be true to ourselves regardless of what anyone else thinks. When we treat ourselves with respect and take responsibility for our own feelings, we will become our own best friend. Once this happens—no matter who our friends are, our self-esteem will be rock solid.

~

Which friends do I have the most in common with?
Which friends do I have the least in common with?
How do I pick my friends?

~

Social Media

Facebook, Instagram and Twitter are among some of the most popular places to socialize. It can be a lot of fun to post pictures, express ourselves and keep up with what our friends are doing. However, if we're not careful, social media can quickly become a place where we are addicted to checking to see how many "followers" we have or how many people "like" our posts. If we attach our self- esteem to these numbers, we'll be giving people the power to affect us based on the push of a button. Self- esteem cannot be built from interacting with a screen. Social Media is not real life. It's entertainment. We must keep this in perspective so that we clearly know the difference between what is real and what is not.

~

How many hours in a day do I spend on social media?
Do I believe that I'm balanced in this area of my life?

~

Building Self Esteem

A person with high self- esteem stands out. Being honest, kind, helpful, respectful, and courageous and doing the right thing when no one is looking are all great ways to build self-esteem. Being selfish, lazy, rude or dishonest are all behaviors that take away our self-esteem. Building self-esteem comes over time, not overnight. However, when we are consistently building self-esteem, we might find it more and more uncomfortable to act out in negative behaviors. Eventually the consequences for these behaviors will be too painful for us. This is when we move from building self –esteem, to having self-esteem. It's a beautiful process.

~

Who do I know with self-esteem?
How can I tell that this person has self-esteem?

~

CHAPTER 42: *Healthy Choices*

The Basics

What does making "healthy choices" mean? Washing our hands before we eat. Eating fruit instead of candy. Going to bed instead of playing on the computer or watching T.V. all night, flossing and brushing our teeth twice a day, putting down the video games and reading a book instead. These are all choices we can make on a daily basis to be healthier people, feel better, and be good examples for the people around us.

~

What are some healthy choices that I already make?
What are the healthy choices that I need to work on?
Why is it important to make healthy choices?

~

Being Sick

It's so miserable when we get sick. Even a little cold can ruin our plans for the day. Some people have illnesses like allergies that can't be helped. But there are things we can do to stay as healthy as possible. Eating foods that are rich in vitamins and minerals can help fight off illness. We can also take vitamins every day. Bundling up during cold, wet, or windy weather is always a smart move. Making sure we get enough sleep and drinking lots of water will help hydrate our bodies and keep our insides working better. If we don't want to be sick, then we need to participate in staying healthy.

~

How would I describe my health? Am I strong? Energetic? Tired?
What can I do to be a healthier person?

~

Healthy Relationships

If we want to have healthy relationships, we have to attract healthy people into our lives. To attract healthy people, we have to be healthy ourselves. If we are bossy and pushy, too needy and clingy, or irresponsible and unfocused … we are not going to attract healthy people. Many times our bad habits can push people away before they really get to know us. Working on ourselves is a healthy choice. A healthy relationship is one where there is equality and respect. We should learn to be good listeners. Try to be supportive of others' ideas. Choose our words carefully. Be consistent and reliable. These are all qualities of someone who will attract healthy relationships.

~

What are my best qualities? What are my worst qualities?
Who do I have the healthiest relationships with? Why?

~

Eating Right!

If eating healthy is a priority for our families, then we probably already know how to eat a balanced meal in moderation. But if our family's main meals come from a drive-thru window … then we may have a challenge in front of us. The biggest challenge of eating healthy means eating from the four major food groups. It's important that we know what they are and what the recommended daily amounts are. The next important step is to make sure we are eating three meals a day, with two snacks in between, if needed. When we wait until we're starving, with nothing prepared, we're bound to go with fast food or something that's quick and probably not good for us. Food is fuel for the body. It gives us the energy to be active. Make sure we plan ahead. It will help us make better choices. Remember, we are what we eat!

~

What foods do I eat regularly?
What foods do I need to eat more of?
What foods should I cut back on?

~

Influence

Friends can influence our lives, which is why it is so important to pick our friends carefully. Hanging out with people who are doing the right thing can help make our lifestyles healthy. Hanging out with people who are getting in trouble will bring trouble our way. What we choose today will definitely affect our futures. When we hang out with people who smoke, drink, and ditch school, even if we're not doing these things, the influence can be a costly one. Unfortunately … we are sometimes judged by the actions of the people we hang with. It's important that our influences, associations, and friendships are healthy.

~

What kind of influence do I have on my friends?
What kind of influence do my friends have on me?

~

The Mind

Our minds are very powerful tools. What we expose our minds to can determine what kind of attitude we have. If everything we listen to is positive and inspiring, then there is a good chance that we will have a positive attitude as we go through life. On the flip side … if what we are listening to is negative and dark, that will eventually begin to shape the way we think. So think about the music we listen to, the movies we watch, and the things we and our friends talk about. Keeping our minds healthy is one of the most important choices we will make.

~

What is my mind exposed to? Is it negative? Or positive?
Why is it healthy to maintain a positive attitude?

~

Our Spirit

Our spirit can be defined as the internal nature of who we are. No matter what it is that we believe in … or what we've been taught to believe in … at some point it is important to nourish our spirit. Religion, yoga, meditation, and even mother earth are all things that we use to nourish our spirits. The spirit must be fed just like the body and mind must be fed. Once we find something that nourishes our spirit … we will always be able to pull ourselves out of negativity and hopelessness. Just like everything else … we will get out of it what we put into it. So we must keep exploring until we discover what makes us feel whole internally … then stick with it. This is probably the healthiest thing we can do for our entire beings. Because whether we realize it or not, every single part of us depends on our spirit to be strong.

~

Who do I know has a strong spirit?
What do I do to nourish my spirit?

~

CHAPTER 43: *S-E-X*

The S Word ... Are We Ready?

Sex is a natural part of life. It is one of the ways two people in love connect and show affection to each other. It can be fun and exciting. It is important to be aware that having sex comes with responsibilities. Some people may think that physical protection is the only protection they'll need. But the truth is that emotional protection is equally as important. When two people who are about to have sex do not have the same goal in mind ... the consequences will be painful for at least one of them. Giving up our virginity is a one-time experience, so it's very important that we're emotionally ready and that our partner cares about us. Having sex for the first time can be something special if we want it to be or it can be a casual encounter ... it's up to us. We should be able to discuss this with our partner. If we can't ... then we are probably not ready.

~

Who have I thought about having sex with?
Am I emotionally prepared?
Do I want to be in love with my partner? Why or why not?

~

Safe Sex

If we really think we are ready and we have talked to our partner about it, we want to make sure we have protected sex. Birth control and condoms are the most common forms of protection. If we are going to use birth control, we will need to see a doctor, have an exam, and get a prescription. If we can't do these things, it's possible we aren't ready. Birth control and protection from sexually transmitted diseases (STDs) are two different things. If we truly practice safe sex, we'll need condoms as well as another form of birth control. If we are going to use condoms, it is important that we know how they work and that we carry them with us. We can not make this our partner's responsibility. It is our responsibility. We should discuss birth control with our partner before the big day.

~

Have I discussed safe sex with a doctor?
Do I know all of my safe sex options?

~

Oral Sex

Oral sex is sex by using our mouths. It can create physical intimacy without intercourse … but it is still sex. Some people lie to themselves by thinking that oral sex doesn't count. Whether we are ready for a committed relationship or just experimenting, all of the same rules apply to oral sex. We should be able to discuss having sex before we actually have it. Oral sex can be satisfying but we still need to be safe, which means that a doctor has seen us and said we and our partners are free of sexually transmitted diseases.

~

Have I discussed oral sex with anyone?
Do I have friends that are having oral sex?

~

Masturbation

By touching ourselves … we can achieve an orgasm and sexual pleasure safely. Masturbating is a way to experience sexual pleasure and release without the commitment of a sexual relationship. It is also a way to think about sexual fantasies without having to be in a sexual relationship before we are ready. Some people may feel embarrassed about masturbation, but it is actually a very normal way to explore our own bodies. As long as we are in the privacy of our own rooms and it is not interfering with our daily responsibilities … there is absolutely nothing wrong with it.

~

Am I embarrassed by masturbation?
Why or why not?

~

The Law!

Having sexual intercourse with a minor is illegal. We and/or our partner can get into serious trouble if we are having sex and one or both of us are not of legal age. There are laws that protect minors. Both people having sex should be of legal age and it needs to be consensual, meaning both people fully agree to have a sexual encounter. If one participant is over seventeen, the partner needs to be over seventeen, too, for it not to be considered rape, so we must make sure we know what we are getting into … and with whom. There is no way anyone fourteen or younger should be having sexual intercourse … it is against the law.

~

Why do I think the law says that both people should be over seventeen?
Do I agree with the law? Why or why not?

~

Sexting

Sexting is when we are having sexually-related conversations, which may or may not include pictures, on the internet or on our cell phones. Many of these types of activities are considered illegal so we must be careful what we send and who we're sending it to. These types of texts or emails, when forwarded to other people, can easily end up in the wrong hands and be very embarrassing for us or life threatening to someone else. People end up killing themselves from embarrassment. Sexting … is very dangerous.

~

Have I ever sent or received a sext?
Have I ever sent something that was meant to be private …
and it ended up in the wrong hands?
How did that feel?

~

Plan it Out

Sometimes what starts out as "fooling around" or "making out" can lead to unwanted and/or unexpected results. When we start kissing … without the intention of going all the way … it will take some serious willpower to stop once things get heated up. Passion becomes confused with love … and before we know it, we're doing something that wasn't planned. It's instinctual to want to finish what we start when it comes to sexual desire. So we must use good sense and not put ourselves into a situation that we haven't planned and can't stop.

The consequences could be extremely painful.

~

Have I ever been in a sexual situation that I hadn't planned?
How did I handle the situation?
How could these things have been avoided?

~

CHAPTER 44: *Drugs*

Trouble

A drug is anything swallowed, smoked, or injected that changes how we feel. When we put something in our bodies that affects how we think and act, we are putting ourselves in danger. It may seem like innocent fun at first, but anytime anyone takes a drug … trouble will soon be on its way. No one is exempt. At the very least, we will not be able to make the same reasonable choices while we are high. Lying, hiding, and sneaking are usually the first behaviors that show up. But if we continue to take drugs, more serious problems, such as stealing and illegal activities will haunt us. And all too often, the end results are serious health problems, overdoses, and sometimes death. None of us ever plan to get into trouble. But bad things happen to good people every day. We don't want it to happen to us.

~

Have I ever been offered drugs?
Why is it a good idea to just say no?

~

Why People Do Drugs

Drugs take us away from our feelings … for the moment. They change the way we view ourselves and others. They give us a false sense of security. Some finally feel like they're a part of something … cool. The problem is that it's not real, it doesn't last, and it is very dangerous. Unfortunately, this awareness usually comes after the consequences. But it doesn't have to. Drug awareness is all around us today. Listen and learn. If we are looking for a way to change how we feel as we go through the awkward stage of being a teen … drugs are not the answer. We can survive our feelings. Feelings won't kill us, but drugs can.

~

What are the hardest feelings I have to deal with?
What are some healthy ways to cope with my feelings?
Who can I talk to about my feelings?

~

Cigarettes and Alcohol

Some people only think of hard-core stuff when they hear the word "drugs." But just because something is legal for adults … doesn't mean it isn't a drug. The most common misconceptions are cigarettes and alcohol. They are both drugs. They are addictive and very dangerous. Part of what makes them dangerous is that they are socially acceptable. But we mustn't be fooled. Alcohol and cigarettes kill many people—innocent people—every year. Second-hand smoke and drunk driving accidents are as big a killer of innocent people as lung cancer and liver disease are to smokers and drinkers. Being able to purchase them from a store makes it easier and more convenient to use these legal drugs, but the harm is just as damaging as buying on a street corner.

~

Why do I think cigarettes and alcohol are socially acceptable?
Do I know anyone who is causing himself or others harm by drinking or smoking?
How can I help?

~

Being Addicted

Being addicted to something is no joke. And it can happen to us before we know it. When we put something in our bodies over and over again, our bodies start to depend on it being there. When our bodies don't get it, we start to withdraw (or panic). And now … instead of wanting it … we need it. What happens next? We become obsessed with our drug. Our minds start to plot and justify crazy behavior just to get "one more." Once we're addicted … one more is never enough. The only way out is to stop using the drug and get help.

~

Do I know of any programs or counselors who can help?
What can I do to make sure this doesn't happen to me?

~

How to Get Help

There are many programs available to help people get off drugs. Drug addiction is so common today that schools, hospitals, churches, and even many work places offer help. The key to getting off drugs is that we must want help and being willing to accept help by doing something different. This may mean being open-minded to ideas that sound strange and feel uncomfortable. We may try to tell ourselves that we can stop on our own ... just to avoid the embarrassment. But chances are, if we're thinking about whether or not we need help, we probably have a drug problem.

~

How would I know if I had a drug problem?
Why is asking for help so hard for some people?
What does it mean to do something different?

~

When Someone We Know is in Trouble

Watching people we care about suffer is heartbreaking. We may want to help but we just can't reach them. The solution to their problems may seem obvious to us ... but they can't see it. That is the peculiar thing about the disease of addiction ... it makes no sense. It is beyond our control. So what can we do? We can get them information about help that is available. We can also talk to our parents or an adult. We can be compassionate and supportive without being judgmental. But be aware that if they aren't ready for help ... there's nothing more we can do. Be careful ... sometimes offering to help someone in trouble can put us in danger. Even our closest family members and friends can bring us down with them if we allow it. It's never a good idea to spend a lot of time with anyone who is using drugs. Offer to help. If they won't accept it ... walk away.

~

Why is it important to offer help ... then walk away?
What else can we do to be supportive to someone who is suffering from a drug problem?

~

Killing and Destroying Lives

Simply put ... drugs ruin lives, but here a few numbers ... the statistics are staggering. In this country ... 85,000 people are killed by drunk drivers each year. 17,000 people die each year from illegal drug use, and a mind-blowing 400,000 die each year from tobacco use. And these are just the ones who died. 80 percent of the people in prison are there for drug-related crimes. The number of lives that are destroyed because of brain damage, lung damage, and crippling illnesses from drug use blow these numbers out of the water. There is a "domino effect" that is beyond our comprehension when it comes to how many people get hurt when someone decides to use drugs or alcohol. If we are offered drugs, remember we have a choice. We can't do something just because someone says we should. We need to stick to the facts. The risks are high. The consequences are grave. Are our lives worth the risk?

~

What things am I willing to risk my life for?
Do I know anyone who died from a drug or alcohol-related incident?
How often have I heard drugs mentioned in my local news?
Am I choosing to be a part of the problem or the solution?

~

Chapter 45: *Peer Pressure*

What is it?

Our peers are our friends and schoolmates. Peer pressure is when we have the intense need to fit in and be liked by others. Sometimes the pressure comes from friends who try to control us. But most peer pressure is self-imposed, meaning we put pressure on ourselves to try and look and act like our peers. We may think that if we look as cool as someone else, then we'll feel cool. The problem is, the comfortable feeling we're looking for comes over time, not overnight. The awkward, uncomfortable identity crisis we experience as tweens and teens is just a part of growing up. Every kid goes through it, even the cool-looking ones. As we learn to be ourselves, the need to fit in turns into confidence of who we are. The way we dress, the things we like, and our behavior may change, but along the way … it's okay to be us, even if we're not sure who that is.

~

How would I describe myself?
Is my personal style … Casual? Hip Hop? Grunge? Trendy?

~

Am I influenced by peer pressure?

When we know what peer pressure is … our peers won't have as much power over us. We are all somewhat influenced by other people. However, when our likes and dislikes are dictated by someone else, we've gone from being influenced to being controlled. The people we choose to be around should be people who respect us and our own ideas. If we're around them just because they're popular or pretty, then peer pressure is bound to be a part of the friendship. We need to take a look at our current social circles, and then ask ourselves why we like hanging out with them. This will let us know whether we are influenced by peer pressure and if so, by how much.

~

Are my friends popular? How would I describe my friends?
Am I popular? Do I want to be? Why or why not?

~

Being Myself

Deciding not to be influenced by peer pressure doesn't have to be a big deal. We can decide to be ourselves. And then we act like ourselves. Now that sounds simple, but it can be challenging. People are very easily influenced. And everyone wants to be liked. But being liked can't be more important than being ourselves. Knowing that we may not like every person we meet is important … because then we'll understand that it's impossible for everyone to like us as well. Once we accept this, it can relieve some of the pressure we may feel to please other people. We will never please everyone. So we're better off being true to ourselves by being ourselves.

~

What does it mean to be true to myself?
Does it affect me if someone doesn't like me? Why or why not?

~

School

School is usually where we get our first glimpse of peer pressure. It can be very uncomfortable and sometimes painful. Taking a look at the big picture can sometimes help. Remind ourselves that we go to school for the sake of an education. This may or may not make us feel better, but it is the purpose of school. We can also try to find our own place in school. This is our school, too. A school does not belong to any one group of kids … even though it may sometimes seem that way. School can be a very social place, but socializing shouldn't be our priority. We need to find something we like about our school and put our energy and focus there.

~

What are my favorite required classes at school? What are my favorite electives?
Why do I like these classes?

~

How I Say No ... When I've Already Said Yes

Changing our minds can sometimes be more difficult than if we had just said no from the start. But it is possible to do. And we will find that saying no to something we don't want to do will free us from the pressure we feel. Most people will accept no as an answer if we just say it. They may not like it, but they will either move on or stop pushing so hard. And we will feel better about ourselves.

~

What's the last thing I said "yes" to, when I really wanted to say "no"?
Did I do it anyway? Why or why not?

~

I Have a Choice

When we are feeling overwhelmed, it may seem as if our lives will always be like that. But we need to realize that whatever we are going through will pass. We may need to reduce the number of activities we participate in or the number of people we socialize with to get back on track. Our teen years will be very special years for us if we can embrace what they have to offer. They can be the beginning of either a long and exhausting attempt to impress other people ... or an exciting adventure into our future goals and dreams. The choice is ours. Anything that doesn't bring out the best in us, anyone who treats us unkindly or disrespectfully, any behavior or activity that keeps us from being true to ourselves does not belong in our lives. Sometimes cleaning up our lives is all it takes to feel better and give us some hope.

~

Do I have any friends who don't bring out the best in me? Who?

~

Gangs

Gangs are probably the most dangerous examples of peer pressure today. They are in just about every school, neighborhood, and culture in our society. Joining a gang usually begins with pressure from a peer toward someone who's desperate to fit in somewhere. At first, someone may actually feel like a part of something. But it's not a good thing. Gang activity involves aggressive and violent behavior that usually hurts innocent people. Tagging, vandalism, stealing, and fighting over colors, drugs, and territories are just a few things that eventually put gang members in jail. But the trouble doesn't end there. There are as many gangs in jails as are on the streets. Once someone joins or hangs out with a gang, he may never get the chance to change his mind. Gangs are not the answer.

~

Are there any gangs at my school?
Have I ever thought it might be fun or exciting to be in a gang?
Why or why not?

~

CHAPTER 46: *Coping SKILLZ*

What Are Coping SKILLZ?

Coping SKILLZ are the "tools" we use when life gets tough. They are also the tools we use to get over the little roadblocks that sometimes pop up. They are priceless. When a crisis happens … like the death of a loved one, a divorce, or a sudden loss of money, we have to cope with these situations. And to do that we will need to learn some coping SKILLZ. They are like having a survival kit on a hiking trip, but they are for our inner selves. Some people fall apart and crumble the minute something bad happens. Some people simply shut down and others just pretend it isn't really happening. None of these are healthy reactions to a trauma. It's normal to be scared or cry. But at some point … we will need to cope with our reality. That's where our coping SKILLZ come in.

~

What was the last tragic thing that I went through?
How did I get through it?

~

Stay Positive

Surviving a crisis in our lives … is a choice. There is nothing worse than feeling like we are at the mercy of a situation. No situation should ever dictate how we are going to feel. Life is going to happen and sometimes situations just aren't going to go our way. But that shouldn't be a reason to stay in a bad mood or feel sorry for ourselves every day. We can be in charge of our thoughts. One of the most powerful coping SKILLZ is to stay positive, grateful for what we have, and look for the lesson. There is something to learn from every situation.

~

Do I get into a bad mood when things go wrong? Why or why not?
When do I feel sorry for myself?
What can I do to change that thinking?

~

Staying in the Moment

Another great coping skill is "staying in the moment." That means thinking only about what we are doing right now. This skill helps us keep our heads clear. Most of us regret something that already happened or fear something that is going to happen. If we really think about this … neither one of these things is in the moment. Therefore … in the moment … we are safe. Nothing's wrong. We don't need to think about the past or future. We can start by thinking about simple things like … what are we doing … where are we sitting … how are we breathing … right now. This is how we stay in the moment. If we can master this coping skill, we will save ourselves a lot of pain throughout our lives.

~

Why is staying in the moment such a valuable coping skill?
What am I doing at this moment?

~

Talk it Out

Talking about a situation can relieve a lot of pressure and is very, very important. When we decide that we don't want to tell anyone what is going on … it allows the situation to take us hostage. The longer we keep it inside, the more fear we will have about talking to someone about it. Shutting down can make us very sick inside. Remember, we don't have to tell everyone. We just need to find one or two people whom we can trust to listen and help support us through whatever we are going through. Talking it out will take some of the power and fear away.

~

Do I talk about my problems or keep them in?
Whom do I trust to be a good listener? Why does talking it out help?

~

Feelings Change

Some situations can make us feel hopeless. And hopelessness feels like it will never go away. But that's not true. The way we feel today is not necessarily how we will feel tomorrow. This is important to remember because the choices we make today can definitely affect us tomorrow. Before we make any important decisions based on how we are feeling, we need to let some time pass … because feelings change.

~

What was the last situation that made me feel hopeless?
What was the last important decision I made?

~

No Expectations

One of the worst things we can do to ourselves is to plan our future with an expectation. That means when we have plans, we already expect that things will happen they way we planned them. Everyone has hopes and dreams, but when we expect that life should go a certain way, we can cause ourselves serious heartaches. If our expectations of the future are where we put our happiness … we are setting ourselves up to be disappointed. Our happiness should be in the here and now … not in what we want to happen in the future. Life will not always turn out the way we planned it. Life happens the way it happens. So no matter what it is we're hoping for … it's okay to put a plan into action — but beware of expectations — then we won't be disappointed, no matter what the outcome.

~

What are my plans for my future?
What's the difference between hoping and having expectations?
Why is it important to be clear on the difference?

~

Acceptance

Wrapping our hearts and minds around a troubling situation will take a little time and a little work. Sometimes we need to allow ourselves to "feel bad" for a little while. But at some point we need to accept what has happened and move on. The quicker we can do this … the sooner we will feel better. If we are continually resisting the changes in our lives … it will be harder for us to move on. People can be "stuck" for a long time before they realize how long they have been "unhappy." So even though the situation may be very tragic … acceptance will eventually open the door to feeling better.

~

What do I need to get some acceptance of?
Have I ever been stuck in the grieving process?
What things are hard for me to let go of?
How can I use acceptance to get on the other side?

~

Chapter 47: *Eating Disorders*

Anorexia

Trying to define ourselves by how thin we look can very quickly turn into unhealthy behavior. Anorexia is an eating disorder that starts with a person's desire to be thin. It continues with never being thin enough. Anorexics see themselves as overweight even when they are not. Being thin then becomes an obsession. Many girls (and sometimes boys) end up starving to death or becoming very ill. It is a trap. They think they're in control. But once they become addicted to the feeling of not eating … their minds develop a fear of food that begins to control their lives and can eventually ruin it.

~

Do I consider myself overweight? Thin? Healthy?
Do I know someone who might be anorexic? What can I do?

~

Bulimia

Another eating disorder that thrives on being thin is bulimia. This is when a person eats a meal and then makes herself throw up so she won't gain weight from the calories. Bulimia is a sickness, like anorexia, but it is different because the anorexic doesn't want to eat at all, while the bulimic enjoys eating she just won't let herself digest what she eats. But the thought behind it is the same … that somehow our lives will be better if we are thin. It is a lie. This disorder is very hard on our bodies, physically and emotionally. Once the illness has control over us, we can't help but sneak around and tell lies in order to keep it a secret. We can become very sick and the disorder takes over and destroys us.

~

Do I know anyone who is bulimic?
Have I ever tried to make myself throw up? Why or why not?

~

Overeating

The need for instant gratification in our society is insatiable and many of us turn to food to satisfy this need. But "using" food can escalate into compulsive overeating and before we know it … we might be eating against our own will. Being overweight can lead to depression, isolation, and serious health issues. If we are overeating … at some point we will probably be overweight. Learning how to eat in moderation is an ongoing process for many … and is also one of the hardest to master because we have to eat. But we don't have to overeat. Look at our patterns of eating and make the appropriate changes so we can enjoy a long and healthy life.

~

Am I an overeater?
Do I find myself using food for comfort? Why or why not?

~

Getting Help

Admitting that we have a problem is still the best way to start the process of getting help for ourselves. If we're not sure whether or not there is a problem, then we need to talk to someone who cares about us. Tell them about our concerns and ask for their advice. Educate ourselves about the dangers of eating disorders. And then educate ourselves about nutritional guidelines for our age and lifestyle. Help is available all around us … all we have to do is ask.

~

Is it hard for me to ask for help? Whom do I trust to ask for advice?

~

It's Not About Control

Eating disorders may start out as a desire to be thin ... but they quickly turn into a need to be in control. Whether it is under-eating or over-eating, most people experience a false sense of control and may begin to thrive on that feeling, even if it causes them pain in the long run. People like to believe they're in control. If we can accept our lives exactly the way they are ... the good and the bad, we won't have a need to control anything.

~

Does my life seem out of control?
Is there one area in particular I wish I could change? Why or why not?
Why is it important to accept my life exactly the way it is?

~

The Competition

With such an enormous focus on "size" in today's society, it's pretty challenging for a teen not to develop an eating disorder. No matter what we're into ... sports, dance, cheer, or just looking fashionable and trendy, our society is obsessed with the idea of thin. But there is a difference between being fit and just being thin. We all have our own unique build. Genetics determine how we are built. Some people have larger frames and simply aren't meant to be tiny people. It's insane for someone who has a muscular build to try to be the same size as someone who has a slight build. Both people can be fit ... meaning not underweight or overweight ... but just right for their size. Competing with someone else to reach a number, either on the back of our jeans or on the scale, will eventually take us down the wrong road. Compete with ourselves to eat healthy and be fit so we can honor the bodies we were born with.

~

Have I ever been fixed on the idea of wearing a certain size?
Do I compare my body to my friends' bodies?
What does being healthy and fit mean to me?

~

Be in the Solution

Doing things differently after we've been on the 'dark side' of an eating disorder is a slow healing process. We might have to make some tough changes to stay healthy. These changes may include changing the places where we hang out and the people we hang out with. It may seem uncomfortable at first, but just like any change it will become routine after a while. Making our health a priority is important because if we don't … we may slip back into our old ways. Once we have an eating disorder we will always have an eating disorder. Much like drug addiction, we will need to stay on top of it. But it doesn't have to haunt us for the rest of our lives. There are plenty of happy, healthy people around us who once struggled with eating disorders. They simply take care of themselves today. They don't wear signs on their foreheads and we wouldn't know their stories unless we knew them personally. But they're out there. If they can do it, we can, too.

~

Do I know anyone who has healed from an addiction or eating disorder?
How did he or she do it?
Why are lifestyle changes important for the healing process?

~

CHAPTER 48: *Money*

Don't Let it Define Us

We need money to survive. Food, clothes, and shelter are all things that we can't have without money. But happiness cannot be bought … because it's free. When people start to believe that they need money to be happy, money starts to control them. Once this happens … there is never enough money. Money is a tool that we need to support us through life but it should not define who we are or whether or not we're good enough. Some people judge and are judged by how much money they have. Don't get caught in this trap.

~

Do I know anyone who is defined by how much money they have?
Have I ever felt judged because I didn't have enough money?

~

Have a Plan

The plan for handling our cash should be in place before we actually start earning it. And there are several ways to come up with a budget. First, it's always a good idea to discuss a plan with our parents. They should be able to help put a budget together. A basic formula is to commit to saving a certain amount, use a portion for entertainment, and give back in some way. Whether we choose to donate to a worthy cause or help someone in need, being caring enough to help others will benefit us in the long run. The key to success is to be responsible, create a budget, and stick to our plan.

~

What is my plan for handling money?
Am I responsible with money?
What do I think happens to people who don't have a plan?

~

Save Some

Many times people misuse their money or act irresponsibly. Saving a portion of our money each and every time we earn some … will help us in a couple of ways. It builds self-esteem and provides some security in case of a rainy day. When we are able to save some money, we'll feel good about ourselves. Using self-control with our spending habits will help create good habits in other areas of our lives as well.

~

Do I have any money saved? Why or why not?

~

Give Some Away

Some people will tell us that helping others is the reason we are on this planet. And some people actually dedicate their entire lives to helping others. We may be one of them. It is an awesome purpose in life to help those less fortunate … either with our time or our money or both. But even if helping others isn't our only purpose in life, it should always be a part of our lives. Helping others can add so much joy to our lives and to the lives of those who we are helping.

~

Why do I think helping others is important?
Who has been helpful to me? How have they helped?

~

Spend Some

We all have needs and wants … and keeping those straight throughout our lives can be like walking on a balancing beam. Our needs should always come first when learning to be responsible with money. It's important to pay bills on time and not take on new bills that we can't afford. After we pay our bills, we can consider our wants. But keep in mind that spending money is a powerful feeling and many people have had to learn that the hard way. If we find ourselves buying things just so we can spend … it may be time to take a break and seek some advice.

~

Do I enjoy spending money? Why or why not?
Am I afraid to spend money? Why or why not?

~

Know Our Limits

We all want to live a good life. And one surefire way to do that is by living within our means. There is nothing less satisfying than always being broke and waiting for our next paycheck. So as we enter into the world of earning … we need to know our limits. It's insane to start earning money without having a plan. Decide on how much we're going to save and put that away first. We will quickly see who's in charge … us or our wants. If we want to control our money responsibly, then we should know in advance how much we can afford to spend … and then stick to it. Otherwise, our money will control us. And that can lead to a lot of disappointments down the road.

~

Have I ever gotten carried away with money?
Do I end up borrowing from people until payday?

~

Cash is King

Cash is king is an old saying that means … there is no better way to pay for something than with cash. The truth in the world of finances is … if we can't pay cash for it … then we really can't afford it. Credit cards and borrowing for purchases may seem like a good idea but once we have credit card payments or we're always paying someone back what we owe, those responsibilities can be overwhelming. When we can actually practice the discipline to save for something that we want … and pay cash for it, we will begin to see the power behind having cash. On the other hand, when we use credit for purchases to satisfy our instant gratifications, we have fallen into an ugly cycle. So beware!

~

Why do I think some people get into trouble with credit cards?
What does the term "instant gratification" mean to me?

~

CHAPTER 49: *School*

A Melting Pot

America is sometimes referred to as "a melting pot" because of the diversity; there are so many differences. And we may find the same thing on a smaller scale in school. Whether we attend public or private school, we will probably be exposed to many different types of people. Some people will dress differently, act differently, and even observe different holidays. When we look for the differences between people, we're sure to find them. And if we judge people based on our differences, we'll end up pushing people away. However, if we embrace the differences … we could learn some very fascinating facts about other cultures, possibly make some new friends, and above all find out that we all feel the same on the inside.

~

Are there people of different races and cultures at my school?
Have I ever tried to be friends with someone who's different from me?
Why or why not?

~

Play it Smart

On average we spend thirty-five hours a week at school, which is a big chunk of our lives. So it probably makes sense to make the most of our time at school. Some days we might just be waiting for the bell to ring but school shouldn't just be a place to hang out while our parents work. School could be that place where we find our strengths and plan a future. This is where many different aspects of our lives will unfold. By playing it smart in school and paying attention to what's going on … the possibilities are endless.

~

Where do I see myself in the future?
What classes at school interest me?

~

School is Cool

One day we will look back at our school years as some of the best years of our lives. Until then … school may sometimes seem like a burden. The truth is … that when we are making the most out of school … school is cool. There are so many different groups to sign up for. Sports, glee club, cheerleading, debate team, and theater are just a few of the exciting things we get to take full advantage of at school. Where else can we go and do so much in one day? We will only get out of it … what we put into it.

~

Am I taking advantage of everything my school has to offer? Why or why not?
What can I sign up for that would make school more fun?

~

Fitting in

We all have days where we feel like we don't fit in anywhere. Sometimes it could simply be our mood that day … but often we just haven't found a group of friends that we're comfortable with. In school it's common to be attracted to the "cool" kids. However, it's important that we actually like the people that we're hanging around with. It's also a plus if they like us too. There are a few things to consider before picking a group of friends. Age, culture and common interests are usually the normal considerations. We may forget to include values and lifestyles. If we don't share the same values as our friends … we will never really fit in with them because we will never be able to be ourselves. We can only fake our way for so long. If we continue to look for people like us, and be ourselves in the process, we are bound to fit in somewhere.

~

What are my values?
What are my interests?
Do my friends share my same beliefs?

~

The School of Life

Usually when we think of an education we think of school. However, there are many ways that everyday life can give us an education. Some of us will get an education from top schools around the world. Others will get a free education from the library. But never underestimate the power of learning from our own mistakes and the mistakes of others. Life is a never-ending learning experience. Remember there is an education waiting wherever we choose to look for it.

~

What am I learning about life that I didn't learn in school?
What mistakes have I made that I know will help me in the future?

~

Helping Others

School is a great place to help others. Many schools have fundraisers to help the school or a family in crisis. Helping others is a valuable asset and a great way to show appreciation for what we have. Volunteering to tutor students or helping the staff with filing or making copies, are all things that will enhance our work ethic and build self-esteem too.

~

How do I think helping others helps me?
Where am I needed the most at my school?
How can I help?

~

Social SKILLZ

School is more than a learning center for math and science. It is also where we begin to learn social SKILLZ. Everything from following rules to working in groups will somehow affect our future socially. Learning to get along with people, no matter how different they are, will play a huge role in how society views us as adults. These social SKILLZ are just as important as reading and writing are … especially when we enter the workplace. When we think about it … where else would we learn these things?

~

Why do I think it's important to learn social SKILLZ?
Why do I think school is the best place to learn them?

~

CHAPTER 50: *Safety*

Safety First

Safety should always come first. Remember when we were younger and we were always being told things like … look both ways before crossing the street. Or … don't talk to strangers. We are told these things repeatedly so we can be safe. However, as we get older, some of us start to believe that nothing bad can ever happen to us. We may forget that safety should always come first, no matter how old or smart we are. So the next time we hear voices from our past telling us to be careful … maybe we should listen … just to be on the safe side.

~

What are some of the "safety first" things that I recall hearing as a child?
Do I still practice safety rules I was taught when I was a child?

~

Be Accountable

We've probably heard someone say … better safe than sorry. That means when we have a choice to do something that might risk our safety, we should probably err on the side of caution. In other words … be careful! It is our responsibility to be aware of our surroundings, be where we say we are going to be and to always let someone know if our plans change. As we get older, the idea of having to be accountable for our whereabouts may irritate us. But we shouldn't confuse independence with rebellion. Making healthy choices is about independence. Lying about our whereabouts or what we're really doing is rebellion. And there will be a price. There are many dangers in the world and we hear about horrible things happening every day. Being accountable to our family and friends, staying aware of our surroundings, and using common sense will help keep us safe.

~

How do I participate in my own safety?
What does being accountable mean to me?
How do I stay aware of my surroundings?

~

Common Sense

There are some very basic safety measures that fall under common sense. Things like buckling our seatbelts and locking the door when we leave the house we probably do automatically. But for some of us, common sense doesn't kick in so easily … especially when dealing with social decisions. For example … getting into a car with someone who's been drinking or going to the mall with friends who might be stealing is an absolute "no thanks" when using common sense. But when we add peer pressure or worse … bullying, common sense can fly right out the window and usually our safety goes with it. It's important to remember everything we are learning and apply it to all situations we're faced with. This is taking common sense to a whole different level.

~

What does common sense mean to me?
Why do safety and common sense go together?
When's the last time I used common sense?
When's the last time I didn't use common sense?

~

Good Judgment

Having good judgment may not come overnight but if we pay attention to the lessons that are parents and coaches are trying to teach us our good judgment can grow over time. Most of us probably don't realize how much we jeopardize our safety with poor judgment … until we have consequences behind it. Good judgment usually includes a "gut check." That means if something makes us feel uneasy, then it is probably not a good idea. We all have something that we wish we could have done differently; that's just a part of life. Practicing good judgment requires practice. That means we are not always going to get it right but we probably have a better chance of staying safe if we have good judgment.

~

What is the last big decision I made? Was I using "good judgment"?
How does "good judgment" help keep me safe?

~

Help Someone … Tell Someone

If we think someone is being abused by someone else or hurting themselves, help them … tell someone. Abuse is never okay and sometimes people are too ashamed to let anyone know what they're going through. If we know of abuse and we're not saying anything … we're hurting the situation rather than helping. It's important to ask someone who can actually help, like a parent, a counselor, or a group leader. Most adults have the experience and the ability to come up with a solution that is best for everyone. But no one can change a problem until they know about it.

~

Do I know someone who may need help?
Who can I go to for advice?

~

Be Prepared

This is the motto of the boy/girl scouts. Being prepared means we know in advance how to handle an emergency situation. In school, fire drills and self-defense classes are our first introductions to preparation. Common sense says … if we're prepared when something goes wrong, there's no need to panic. There are lots of things we can do to educate ourselves in case of an emergency. Getting our families involved in Neighborhood Watch is a start. Learning CPR and how to use a first aid kit may also come in handy some day. We can never be too prepared.

~

Why do I think it is important to be prepared?
What kinds of groups can I get involved in to practice safety?
Who do I know is already prepared regarding safety?

~

Strangers

The best defense against strangers is not to talk to them. Unfortunately, there are people in this world who are sick and might want to hurt us. So, we must always be aware of our surroundings and have a plan … in case we are ever approached by a stranger. The buddy system has been successful for many years. Two heads are better than one. Most times, a stranger with bad intentions won't even approach someone unless she is alone. We must make sure we stay aware of who's nearby and never walk anywhere by ourselves.

~

Do I ever walk to the park, school, or the store by myself?
What is my plan if I get approached by a stranger?
Do I have a buddy system? Why or why not?

~

CHAPTER 51: *Helping Others*

Volunteering

Volunteering our time to help others builds character and can make us feel good, too. There are always plenty of opportunities to be of service. Maybe our local church needs someone to help clean up. Maybe our school is looking for people to help tutor the younger ones. If someone spills something … help them clean it up. If we get to the door and someone is walking in behind us … hold the door open for that person. No matter how small the task, volunteering to help without being asked will make us feel good about ourselves and show our appreciation for our community.

~

What do I do to help people out?
What more can I do?

~

Thinking of Ourselves Less Often

It's human nature to think about ourselves, our wants, our problems, and our futures. But for most of us, this is not when we are at our best. When we think of ourselves less, we are likely to think more about helping others. When we are doing for someone else, no matter how small, it will bring out the best in us. Helping others will give our lives a sense of purpose. And it's possible that we might stumble onto something that we're good at … as well as easing someone's struggles. But it starts with thinking about ourselves less. When we catch ourselves wallowing in "me, myself and I," we need to take a look around and help someone.

~

Do I spend a lot of time thinking about myself? Why or why not?
How much time of my week is spent helping others?

~

Be Humble

It's a real turn-off when someone does something nice for someone and then tells everyone about it. Although there are a few people who help others without the need to be noticed, that is not the norm. Most of us want to be patted on the back for doing something good. Unfortunately, this takes the good out of the deed. Not for the receiver but for the person doing the giving. The whole idea behind helping others is to 'get out of ourselves'. If we need people to know how great we are then we've just made it all about us. Being humble means that we're willing to do a good deed without any recognition for it. The fact that we helped someone in need should be more than enough for us to feel good about who we are. Don't let our egos ruin it for us.

~

Have I ever done something nice and then wanted everyone to know?
Why do I think people want to be patted on the back for helping someone?

~

Co-dependency

We may love to help others. Some people devote their entire lives to serving others. The feelings of being needed and appreciated are powerful ones. So is the feeling of importance. If we find ourselves starting to think that none of these people will be okay without us … then we may be co-dependent. This means that we can't be okay unless they are okay. And our "help" becomes control. This is very dangerous for both the helper and the person being helped. Being co-dependent can be a hard habit to break. The best way around this is to help others without expecting anything at all in return. Give freely and selflessly. And know we can't change anyone.

~

Why is it important to give selflessly?
What is the difference between giving freely and giving with an expectation?

~

Compassion

Having compassion for someone who is hurting comes straight from the heart. To be able to feel the struggles that someone else is going through and have the desire to be there for them is practicing compassion. It is how we help each other. It is what we need from each other. When we see someone struggling with something, we should not judge them ... show them compassion. It can change who we are from the inside out.

~

What is the difference between compassion and judgment?
When have I practiced compassion rather than judgment?
Who was the last person I showed compassion to?

~

Giving

It is better to give than to receive. There is always someone less fortunate who can benefit from our generosity. There are some people who put money in the basket at church, or generously donate when they hear about a fundraiser at a school or community center. These people will get back what they gave ten times over. It may come in a simple "thank you" at first, but eventually they will receive so much more than their initial donation. It has no explanation ... it just is. When we have it to give ... share it. If everyone followed this simple suggestion ... no one would ever go without.

~

Am I a generous person? Why or why not?
Who are the generous people in my life?

~

Sacrifice

Sometimes helping others requires a sacrifice. It's not always easy or convenient. In fact, sometimes it's inconvenient. If someone is sick or can't do things for themselves, we may have to give up something we'd rather be doing in order to help. We might have to give up a night out with friends or even sacrifice a whole week's worth of our free time. When we make a sacrifice to help someone else … it's okay if it feels like a burden at first. We're not horrible people because we'd rather be doing something else. However, we won't feel very good about ourselves if we allow these feelings to keep us from helping. We help each other out of love and compassion regardless of what we have to give up to do it. We may not feel all warm and fuzzy right away, but at the very least … we will have shown ourselves what we're made of. For this alone we can be proud.

~

What's the last helpful thing I did that I'm proud of?
What's the last sacrifice that someone made for me?

~

CHAPTER 52: *Staying in the Moment*

What it Means

Staying in the moment means that we make a decision not to worry about the past or the future. When we stay in the moment everything is okay because we are only focused on whatever we are doing right now. This is a very simple concept to understand, but not that easy to do. The mind is so powerful that we can think about something for long periods of time before we are even aware of it. As we go through our day … we must try to be aware of how often we're either afraid that something might happen or regretting something that's already happened. These are the times that we're not staying in the moment. The truth is that we can't do anything to change the past or the future; we can only find freedom in the moment.

~

Am I worried about something that hasn't happened yet?
Am I regretting something that has already happened?
Why is staying in the moment so freeing?

~

Life Happens

Life doesn't always happen as we plan. Some days we may be pleasantly surprised at how well things are going and other days it may feel as though the bottom has fallen out. Life happens as it happens. It has no emotion. Life isn't bad or good. It just is. It is the way we see things that make them bad or good. If we can go through our day without labeling everything as good or bad and try to learn something from each situation … then life can unfold exactly the way it should.

~

Do I view my life as good or bad? How?
How can I change the way I view my life?
What are the benefits of changing the way I look at things?

~

Free from Fear

For most of us, fear usually comes in the form of 'what ifs'. What if I get a bad grade? What if my best friend doesn't forgive me? What if I don't get what I want? Our minds dwell on these kinds of questions with no other purpose than to fill us with more and more fear. There is never an answer to the 'what ifs' … it's simply wasted time. When we stay in the moment, remembering that we are powerless over any outcome, we can be free from fear, and the 'what ifs' no longer matter. And we will find out the answer to our questions … when we find out and not a second before. So whether the outcome is what we wanted or what we were dreading … we don't ever have to be tortured by fear anymore.

~

What does it mean to be free from fear?
Why is it useless to worry about what might happen?

~

Making Mistakes

Everyone makes mistakes. And mistakes can be embarrassing … especially when we are making them. But mistakes happen. As life unfolds around us, we will learn many valuable lessons. Some of the most valuable lessons will come from our mistakes. When we try and learn from our mistakes, we are taking advantage of the moment, getting away from the feeling of embarrassment and confirming what we don't want to do next time.

~

What's that last embarrassing mistake I made?
What did I learn from it?

~

Don't Plan the Outcome

Staying in the moment is a way to stay peaceful inside. It should never be used as an excuse. We must still take responsibility for our past actions, just as we are responsible for setting goals and planning for our futures. However, once we have done our best to put things in place … our part is done. The outcome of any situation is out of our control. That's when we choose to stay in the moment and let nature take its course. We plan for the future with hope not expectations. Planning the outcome is a recipe for disaster. We will always be disappointed if we can't learn when to let go.

~

Why is it a bad idea to plan an outcome?
How do I know when to "let go"?
What does it mean to "let go"?

~

It's a Choice

One of the most powerful things that we will ever do is make a choice. The freedom to choose is something that everyone has. What we choose can be the difference between hope and hopelessness, peace and turmoil … and even life and death. Some of us are convinced that things like fear of the future or regret of the past … are out of our control. But the truth is … that just like we choose what clothes to wear, what we're going to eat and who our friends are … we can practice choosing to stay in the moment any time we want. Everyday life will give us another opportunity to get better at it. Once we can master making that choice we will truly be home free.

~

What does the "freedom to choose" mean to me?
What are the benefits of choosing to stay in the moment?

~

How?

At this point we all understand the concept of staying in the moment, but some of us might be thinking … "How do I do it"? Here's how. The next time we catch ourselves worrying or feeling sorry for ourselves … stop. Take a breath and ask ourselves these questions: Where am I right now? What am I doing right now? Who am I interacting with right now? Am I sitting or standing right now? What time is it right now? And so on. These simple questions will help to shift the focus off of our worries and into the moment. We may have to repeat this a few times; however, when we continue to remind ourselves of what's happening in the moment … eventually our minds will stay in the moment. We should give it a try. We have nothing to lose.

~

Am I willing to try something different?
Do I think "outside of the box"? Why or why not?

~

About the Authors

Growing up in a very dysfunctional home, Revel turned to drugs and alcohol to help her cope with the feelings. At the age of fifteen, she left home and dropped out of school. She had virtually no life SKILLZ and struggled to survive. Many years later and after a lot of tough life lessons, she started to recover. She finally learned that even though bad things happen—and they do—life is a precious gift. Wanting to find a way to share this gift with her children, she decided to write a book that could help them learn to live life with a set of SKILLZ that she didn't have access to as a young person growing up. The open communication that she has with her children today is a direct result of practicing SKILLZ in the home, where everyone has a voice and can share their feelings openly and honestly.

~

Wynter was taken away from her mentally ill mother at a very young age. She was placed into the foster care system and grew up without a sense of family or a safe place to freely share her feelings. Wynter spent the majority of her teenage and young adult years numbing her pain with drugs. Thankfully, she found recovery from her past and began to bring closure to a lot of the issues that led to her low self esteem.

Today, as the adoptive parent of two beautiful children, Wynter has begun a deeper level of healing. When presented with the opportunity to write this book, Wynter jumped at the chance to be a part of something extraordinary. By using SKILLZ as a vehicle for communication in her own home, Wynter continues to be inspired by her children's enthusiasm to discuss the topics in SKILLZ and learn more about each other. The use of this book has become a regular guide to communication that is bringing her family closer every day.